TOMORROW'S LEADER

HOW THE
BEST LEADERS
BECOME BETTER
IN A FAST-CHANGING WORLD

JOHN LAURITO

Marcus Webb, editor/researcher

Dedicated to my kids Nick and Sky, my two most supportive fans, my toughest critics, and my favorite test audience.

Special thank you to Marcus Webb who so masterfully, and artfully, brought my ideas and story to life.

ISBN (Print): 978-1-09837-408-2
ISBN (eBook): 978-1-09837-409-9

ABOUT THE AUTHOR

Through his two decades running organizations, John Laurito has had a passion for learning and teaching top-level leadership. Answering questions like, "What makes the very best leaders so good? How do they influence others (and in some cases, millions of people) to achieve great things or to unite behind one cause or vision? How can one person have so much impact on the world around them?"

Today John shares his expertise on stages all across the world and with companies across the globe that want to develop the very best leaders. He regularly speaks at universities, companies, organizations, conferences and business events on topics ranging from Leadership to Personal Achievement.

As a successful leader himself, John has run several organizations, specializing in "turnarounds"... leading four different organizations through major change and transformation.

Most recently, he served as President & CEO of Concord Wealth Management, the Boston Agency of Penn Mutual Life Insurance Company for seven years. John led the agency to more than triple its size, garnering recognition as Boston Globe's Top Places to Work for multiple years and Expertise' Best Financial Advisors in 2017 (Top 17 out of 170 firms). Penn Mutual recognized the agency's success with the President's Award two consecutive years, the Excellence Award three consecutive years, along with recognizing three of his front line leaders with Manager of the Year for the last five years.

Prior to Penn Mutual, John spent 18 years with Ameriprise Financial in various roles from financial advisor, Field Vice President, and Regional Vice President. He earned the Outstanding Leader Award and Diamond Ring Club honors, through numerous accomplishments including bringing the Hartford, CT office from #100 to #1 in the country under his leadership.

John graduated from Rutgers University with a BA in Economics. He currently resides in North Carolina with his two children Nick and Skylar.

TABLE OF CONTENTS

CHAPTER 1

Whether you realize it or not, you're a leader

You lead yourself, every hour of every day – with every decision you make, and with every action you take.

It was every public speaker's worst nightmare. And it was happening to me.

Without a doubt, the most uncomfortable moment in my life occurred when I was 33 years old. By then I had been a successful financial advisor for 7 years and then was promoted to be a leader (managing executive). After 4 years, I was running the Hartford, Connecticut office for my company, one of America's largest financial services firms.

In one short year, I had helped transform our Hartford branch from one of the worst performers in the country (ranked #100 out of 110) to one of the best: we ranked in the Top 10. Eventually I helped our office reach #1 in the nation.

So when the Regional Vice President of our company called a meeting, and I was invited to make some remarks during a big gathering of executives and employees, it should have been a proud moment for me.

It was anything but.

The audience consisted of about 70 management executives who worked in our wealthy, upscale region. I knew every single one of them. The Regional Vice President spoke first; my direct supervisor spoke next. I knew that I was going to be third.

At first, I was looking forward to it. But as I sat in the audience, waiting to be called up to the stage, I felt my body temperature rising. My neck began to tingle with a flushing, hot, prickly feeling. It spread to my arms and my head. I could feel this thing building as it was getting closer and closer to the moment for me to speak.

The moment arrived. I was invited to say a few words about how we had achieved our remarkable turnaround.

I stood up, and as I walked up the aisle, my breathing became forced and shallow. I struggled to make my lungs take the next breath.

I stepped on stage, went to the podium, turned and faced the audience. And then it broke over me like a tidal wave.

A panic attack.

This was not a slight case of nerves. I am talking about a full-blown, *"heart pounding out of your chest,"* dry-mouthed, flop-sweat, PANIC ATTACK. I am a pretty big, athletic guy and people say that I normally project self-confidence. But at that moment, my face was turning bright red – and I knew it. I could feel my cheeks burning, my forehead burning, and my ears burning. Rivers of sweat rolled off me.

I felt as if someone were strangling me! I could not get a single word out of my mouth -- and believe me, I tried. I just stood there, staring stupidly at the audience, looking helplessly at all those people I knew -- gripping the podium with both hands like a drowning man clutching at a life preserver, and wishing that I could disappear.

The seconds were ticking by in silence, and with every tick of the clock my problem was spiraling out of control. My temperature was going up and up. The amount of air in my lungs (and probably the amount of oxygen going to my brain) was going down and down. By now it was almost zero.

The audience – my friends, colleagues and superiors – all stared at me, wondering what was the matter with me. My boss frowned, as if he wanted to ask the person sitting next to him, "What the hell is wrong with John?"

At the time, I could not have told him, even if I had possessed the power of speech.

Oh, I recognized the symptoms. I had been having panic attacks since 8th grade. And, although I had developed a few rudimentary tricks on my own to calm myself down, I had never talked to a doctor or a therapist about my problem. I had never even read a book on the subject.

And so I had no idea there was a name for this terror that flooded over me whenever I became hyper self-conscious that I was the focus of attention. Or when I suddenly realized that I was in the middle of a crowd, even if they were all paying attention to other people and doing other things.

At that moment in the Hartford office, the only thing I could think to do was to turn my back to the audience so I would not have to look at all those staring eyes.

Behind me stood a whiteboard, and I grabbed a magic marker and just started writing like crazy. To this day, I have no idea what I was writing on that board. I was blindly charging forward, buying time, trying to relax myself, trying to think.

But my condition kept growing worse and worse. I felt like my shirt was shrinking. I turned back around as if to address the audience, but at this point my heart was racing like crazy -- probably north of 150 beats a minute -- and I could see that all those people were legitimately concerned about me. Some of them were probably wondering if I were having a heart attack.

I was plummeting out of the sky, heading for a spectacular crash. *I was completely in the grip of this thing, and there was absolutely nothing I could do to control it*. Instead, it had complete control of me, and I was totally helpless.

In the past, the only tactic I could figure out when I got like this was to get the hell out of there -- get away by myself – escape to a bathroom, an empty classroom, or outside – anyplace I could be alone -- and wait until the terror passed. Wait until my heart started working normally again. Wait until I could breathe and speak and think again.

I had no choice! I had to get out of there! Go! Go! GO!

I dropped the magic marker, leaped off the stage, and bolted out of the room.

Even in the moment, as I fled down the corridor outside the meeting room, I was thinking that this nightmare would have been easier to live with, if my breakdown had taken place in front of a roomful of strangers. But these were people I knew, and who all knew me. They were people whose respect and cooperation I depended on. Quite a few of them were people I liked. Good grief, what would they think of me now?

I raced to the men's room because that's all I could think of. I locked myself in a stall and tried to get control of my breathing.

In another minute or so, I heard the outer door opening and a bunch of guys coming into the restroom. They must have paused the program and told everyone to take a break. They probably didn't know what else to do. But hiding in my stall, I could hear them all coming into the bathroom and I'm thinking, *"Oh my God, they all know I'm in here!"*

I decided to make noises like I was throwing up in the toilet. It was the only cover story I could think of. I thought, "I'll just tell everyone I was sick to my stomach," and after a few minutes, when I felt closer to normal, I emerged from the bathroom and that is exactly what I said.

I guess they believed me. But when I finally went home that night, I knew that I could not go on like this.

Hitting bottom, bouncing back

My panic attack that day turned out to be a major turning point in my life. As a matter of fact, it became an unexpected springboard to tremendous personal and professional growth.

When I had the time to sit down quietly and think clearly about my problem, I knew the worst had happened. I had screwed up in front of the company President, in front of my boss and in front of all my colleagues. Somehow, hitting that definitive low point gave me the ability to see and think objectively about myself and my situation.

On the one hand, I knew that I was achieving real success at my company, and was on the brink of what could be far greater success.

At the same time, I realized that unless I got my "episodes" under control, they would be a severe limiting factor -- not only in my career, but in my life. Feeling helpless and humiliated triggered a lot of anger in me. This was compounded by a lot of frustration, embarrassment, and a host of several other negative emotions.

I decided this was a problem I had to solve. I could no longer just "live with it" and hope it would not return, or that its manifestations would be mild. I faced the fact that it would return, and apparently it would keep getting worse until it ruined my career and damaged my life -- unless I acted.

At that moment I gave myself a mission. I told myself that I would have to try to figure out how to overcome these episodes. And in that moment, I began to practice (and learn) the art of self-leadership.

How I turned my stumbling block into a steppingstone

To make a long story short, I never did consult a doctor or read a book about panic attacks. Again, for many years I didn't realize these episodes were considered a medical or psychological condition that had a standard diagnosis and set of treatments.

But working through the problem on my own, I gradually learned how to prevent my attacks. Oddly enough, much of it involved a kind of reverse psychology.

First I figured out how to *trigger* a panic attack -- by making myself vulnerable and concentrating on scary thoughts and feelings of everyone judging me. By visualizing myself hyperventilating, sweating, turning red, not being able to breathe, feeling my pulse race wildly out of control.

I got pretty good at triggering the onset of a panic attack.

But that sense of being able to control <u>something</u> about these episodes, even if it was how to bring on the very thing I hated, helped me slowly learn how to *prevent* a panic attack. (If you know how to turn a light switch on, I reasoned, you are halfway to figuring out how to turn it off).

Second, I learned the technique of recognizing negative self-talk, which is the voice of doom or the harsh critic you hear in your head. I learned how to argue with those negative voices, and ultimately how to banish them.

Third, I learned to shift my perspective and stop thinking about, "How do I feel? How do I look to other people right now?" Instead, I started asking myself, "How does the other person feel in this moment? What do they want, what do they need? What goal were they focused on before we came into contact, and how can I help them achieve it?"

In addition, I learned to do a lot of meditating and spending quiet time with myself, visualizing the best that could happen, or the things I wanted to happen – not the worst, and not my fears.

All of these coping mechanisms gradually made it possible for me to overcome my tendency to have anxiety attacks. First, I short-circuited the panic attack syndrome in certain minor forms, and every time I succeeded in doing that, it gave me more and more confidence that I would be able to do it again in the future, when facing a larger and more aggressive episode.

In time, that growing sense of confidence spread to other areas of my life. I felt that if I could overcome my worst challenge, the next steps to go forward in my career or my life wouldn't be as hard.

As a result of this entire experience, I changed my life and I gained a tremendous amount of confidence and perspective. I am far happier, less stressed, and fully able to handle the possibility of something that used to scare me to death.

Today I'm no longer in financial services. After a long, enjoyable and highly successful career in that industry, I have built a new career speaking to audiences around the world about leadership. I also work with companies and organizations to transform their leadership teams, and I am an executive coach and trusted adviser to CEOs and organizational leaders. And, I'm the host of the "Tomorrow's Leader" podcast.

Perhaps the most important insight I share with people is that *the first and most important step toward successful leadership is self-leadership.*

How to practice self-leadership

One of the biggest myths about leadership is that it's only for people who hold an obvious, formal "leader" position. Supervisor, manager, executive, department head, chief, the boss, the CEO, the big cheese.

The truth is very different. *Every single person on this planet is a leader.* To begin with, each of us is the leader of ourselves, whether we realize it or not and whether we agree or not.

In addition, millions of people who are not thought of as "leaders" by the world are actually the leader of their family, or their kids, or their circle of friends, their colleagues at work, or their community.

Perhaps their leadership is quiet, and consists of leading by example. But when they act, other people take notice and are influenced. They may follow suit. Perhaps you're the person everyone asks for advice.

Perhaps you don't wait to be asked but speak up and share your views -- and when you do, other people start nodding their heads.

It takes three core elements to have leadership: someone with responsibility and authority; a goal; and a follower or followers.

In a self-leadership situation, who is the person with responsibility?

You -- because you (and only you) have responsibility for yourself and your actions.

In a self-leadership situation, who is the person with authority?

You guessed it: it's you again. You also are the only person who has the authority to decide on what course of action YOU will follow. Self-leadership is more than a business; it's about everything in life. It's how you motivate yourself to do the things you want to do and know that you should do. It usually begins with managing your emotions by reframing your thinking and changing your self-talk — which ultimately controls your actions. In an organization, even if you're the bottom person on the totem pole, where your options may be limited, self-leadership begins with realizing that you do have options. For example...

You can keep your head down, work hard and move up. You can quit and go someplace else. If you're present involuntarily, you can decide to cooperate or you can rebel against the system.

And what does your responsibility to yourself, as the leader of your-self, consist of?

As with every good leader, your responsibility consists of maximizing success for your followers — who, in this case, *also* happens to be you.

Finally, what does success mean in the context of self-leadership?

Defining success is up to you. For some it may be accumulating wealth; for others it might be achieving a certain power or status; and for others, achieving a certain result in the organization or the community.

However you define success, it begins with adopting a <u>goal</u>. When I gave myself the mission of overcoming my panic attacks, that was a goal. It was one of the most important goals of my life.

I led myself by taking responsibility for the problem. I decided it was up to me to solve it -- not up to fate, luck or chance. And, I took the initiative and made serious, steady efforts to learn about the nature of my problem. Next, I practiced using what I learned. Step by step, I led myself from panic to confidence – from fear to enjoyment – and from being almost exclusively self-focused to being largely other-focused.

If you can master the art of leading yourself, then you will be a lot happier and certainly more successful at anything you do. What's more, you will have taken the first giant step toward learning and mastering the art of leadership in any context, with any number of followers.

How Oprah Winfrey got a bear hug on self-leadership, and used failure as a springboard to her astonishing success

I have always found Oprah Winfrey to be an amazing inspirational leader. She is a woman of vision, courage and uncannily wise instincts about what will work and what won't in the business world, coupled to equally profound insights about what is true and untrue about human nature.

When Oprah says, "This is what I know for sure," millions of people lean in and listen closely. She is an influencer. She is a teacher. And in everything she does, says and thinks, she is a leader.

But she did not start out that way. Early in her broadcasting career Oprah Winfrey got hired to co-anchor the local evening news at a TV station in Baltimore – her first big job -- and a few months after that, she got fired.

"I was finally going to have my chance to be like Barbara Walters, who I'd been trying to emulate since the start of my TV career," she admits today. "I tried to sit gracefully like Barbara, and talk like Barbara. The station wanted to change everything about her – her hair, her wardrobe, even her name. "I thought no, it doesn't feel right."

After a few half-hearted attempts to conform to the station's makeover, and after feeling awkward in her own misguided efforts to replicate Barbara Walters, she finally refused to go along.

"I was feeling pretty miserable with myself," she recalls now. Then a light bulb came on. It occurred to her that "I could make a pretty goofy Barbara, or if I could figure out how to be myself, then I could be a pretty good Oprah... I realized I should try being myself."[1]

But who was she? An important clue came from her deep inner drive to make a difference in other people's lives. "I would cover a fire, and then I'd go back to the scene and try to give the victims blankets," she says.

After eight months, management fired her from the evening news. Oprah still had over a year left on her contract, but the station did not want to pay her off, so management demoted her to a far less prestigious job. They made her host of their low-rated local daytime talk show.

Suddenly all the traits that had been flaws in the news business, became virtues in the talk show business. "When you're doing the work you're meant to do," Oprah said later, "it feels right, and every day is a bonus regardless of what you're getting paid." From there Oprah blossomed into the world-class influencer and communicator we all know.

Oprah's story is a prime example of self-leadership. She was her own leader because she took responsibility for her career, blazing a trail to being a different kind of on-air personality, regardless of whether management liked it or not. What's more, she assumed the authority to decide for herself, even when her bosses disagreed.

---

1   Oprah Winfrey, Stanford University Commencement Address, 2008. https://www.youtube.com/watch?v=Bpd3raj8xww&list=PLXD2YeVTziWW92UZiDW-IQH17h4X-7DNx&index=7

Obviously, Oprah did not have any followers (or fans) among station management. But she did have the most important follower in the world: herself! By her own description, she listened to her gut, and she followed its promptings.

Above all, she had a goal. A burning dream. A powerful vision. She was determined to touch people, to connect, to make a positive difference in the lives of others -- even if they were TV viewers whose faces she couldn't see, and whose voices she couldn't hear.

Over the next several decades, as we all know, Oprah Winfrey became a trailblazing pioneer in many ways – broadcaster, empire builder, publisher, founder and creator of a school, and one of the most admired and respected people in the world.

Not everyone can have, or even wants, the astonishing life and career of Oprah Winfrey. But her life teaches us many, many lessons, and all of us can learn from her example and apply those lessons in our own lives.

Leadership, as the "O" model demonstrates, can be fun. It can be spontaneous, instinctive, full of surprises and unexpected journeys. It can be an opportunity for unending personal growth.

Above all, the number-one lesson of Oprah's success comes down to this: _leadership starts with learning how to lead yourself._

Beginning your own personal journey to leadership

From this moment onward, we will take the "JOURNEY TO LEADERSHIP" together. Here's a quick preview of our roadmap.

- In Chapter 2, we'll reveal why <u>leadership is learnable</u>. Do you suspect that you're not cut out for leadership? By the time you finish this chapter, you'll realize that you do have leadership potential. In fact, you may already be exercising leadership without even realizing it.

- In Chapter 3, we'll talk about starting down the path of leadership, and making the trip one small step at a time. We'll focus on a core truth of leadership, which is that small steps add up over time, eventually making an enormous difference.

- We will talk in Chapter 4 about a vital preliminary step: _clearing your path_ of hidden obstacles that may be holding you back.

- In Chapter 5, you will acquire insights that enable you to choose a _great destination_, one that is uniquely inspiring and empowering for YOU.

- Chapter 6 will explain how to respond when you come to a _fork in the road_.

- Hang on tight for Chapter 7, where I will introduce you to some of the _different situations_ that you'll encounter on your personal Yellow Brick Road to successful leadership. In Chapter 8, we'll focus some of the _six leadership styles_ that may be required to lead different teams effectively.

- We will use Chapter 9 to learn how successful leaders tailor their pacesetting, work environments, and management styles to different personalities and groups, including different age groups, people from diverse backgrounds, and varied experience levels.

- In Chapters 10 we'll focus on the _"culture" of leadership_ and how to nurture the _trust_ which is the oil in the engine of progress.

- We'll learn the power of embracing simplicity in Chapter 11, and the high cost of making goals, methods and communication overly complex.

- In Chapter 12, we'll reveal how to _cope with changing times and circumstances_ in a world where change happens faster and faster. and how to survive _storms on the road_ with effective crisis management.

- Finally, in the Afterword we will cross the finish line and enter the winner's circle. You'll get some pointers and places where you can find <u>ongoing additional resources</u> -- including workbooks, podcasts, and personal coaching or workshops by me, to your group or organization.

And so now, ladies and gentlemen, it's your turn. The flag is down. The whistle blows. The starter bell RINGS... and we're off!

What you'll discover at the end of the journey

By the time you reach the end of this book, we will have completed an amazing journey together. In addition, we will have solved one of the most important mysteries of leadership: *Who is Tomorrow's Leader?*

My friend, if you sign up for this trip and whole-heartedly commit yourself to come along with me on this *Journey to Leadership*, then I can reveal the answer to that mystery right now.

TOMORROW'S LEADER IS YOU.

CHAPTER 2

Leadership Is learnable

Leadership is a skill that can be taught -- and YOU can learn it. One important secret is finding your personal leadership style.

Have you ever heard of someone turning down a promotion and a big raise?

Believe it or not, it happens. I saw this occur when I tried to promote a woman I'll call Marcie, one of the best financial advisors who ever worked for me.

It was 10 a.m. on a Monday morning. Marcie entered my office right on time for our appointment. "Good morning, John!"

"Hi, Marcie, thanks for coming. Please sit down."

She sat. Her smile was bright and genuine, but maybe a little anxious around the edges. Apparently, she thought she was about to get a dressing-down for some reason. I tried to correct that impression right away.

"Marcie, I have great news for you. As you know, one of our leadership team is leaving and it's up to me to recommend a replacement. You're the obvious choice."

"Me?" She looked flabbergasted.

"Absolutely. You're the top producer on our team. More than that, you're already practicing leadership. Everybody comes to you for advice and they all look up to you. I think you'd make a great leader."

Marcie's eyebrows knitted together, as if she were thinking very hard. She actually seemed in a bit of distress.

I tried to encourage her by pointing out some obvious benefits. "Of course, the job comes with a substantial increase in salary and earnings potential. You'll have 10 people as direct reports. And, if you do as well as I know you can, in a couple of years you could move up to a regional leadership role. That would mean even higher compensation and more authority."

When she heard the word "authority," Marcie actually flinched. She still didn't say anything.

"Well, what do you think? Are you interested?" I gave her my warmest "you can do it" smile. "I've already told Bill at our regional level that I want to pick you for this advancement, and he agrees with me 100%."

Finally, Marcie spoke. "Thank you so much for thinking of me, John, and please thank Bill too. But I really don't believe I'd be right for that position."

This was not at all what I had expected. Marcie had demonstrated a strong ability to combine career and family, so that was not the issue. I knew she loved working with other people; that was clear from the way she went out of her way to help them. And, she was an effective teacher.

So what was the problem?

"Marcie, I'm sorry to hear that. Is there an issue I should know about? You're not planning to leave the company, are you?"

"No!" she said, looking shocked.

"No health issues, I hope?"

"Oh, nothing like that," she said quickly.

"Good. So can you help me out a bit, maybe explain what you're thinking here? I'd really like to understand."

Marcie hesitated for a long moment. Finally she said, "It's hard to put into words. I guess it comes down to the fact that I just don't see myself as the 'leader type.'"

"What do you mean, the 'leader type'?"

"Oh, you know. I don't have a big commanding personality or anything like that," she said. "You're right, I love talking to people one on one. But I can't see myself taking charge of a group. I like being in the background."

"I see. Anything else?"

"I'm not an expert on every subject that my team would be working on. So how can I tell them what to do? Also, I hate criticizing people. And, if I ever had to fire anyone, I really don't know if I could do that either. I guess I'm just not comfortable with the whole idea of being a leader. I really appreciate your confidence in me," she said. "But I just want to keep my head down and focus on my own contribution."

"I hear what you're saying," I said. "Can we talk about this over a cup of coffee? I really need to understand where you're coming from."

"Sure," she said.

We went to the Starbucks next door, which was practically deserted, and sat down for a chat. In that relaxed atmosphere, I learned some things about Marcie – and about the very different ideas that people have about the meaning of leadership.

What is the essential job of a leader?

I began by asking Marcie what she thought the job of a leader was, and how leaders exercise their authority. And, I asked her to give me an example of someone she knew personally who embodied her conception of leadership.

She began talking about her first boss, a man I'll call Dave. As it happened, Dave had also been one of my first bosses in the company, several years earlier.

It would be an understatement to say that Dave was a tough boss. He was super-critical and relentlessly negative. He seemed to have memorized the entire company manual of policies and procedures. If you failed to cross the slightest "t" or dot the tiniest "i," Dave raked you over the coals.

Back when Dave was a financial advisor himself, he had performed exceptionally well, making tons of money for his clients, himself and the company. But when Dave became a leader, he expected everyone on his team to do things *exactly* the way he had done them, without permitting the tiniest deviation.

Worst of all, Dave routinely ran roughshod over his direct reports. If you turned in a report or completed a project, Dave quickly said the parts that you got right were "fine" -- and then he proceeded to focus at length on the one thing you got wrong. Or, if you didn't get anything wrong, he focused on the one thing he didn't agree with. Frequently, Dave would give you a dressing-down in front of other team members. He seemed to enjoy humiliating people.

Frankly, a lot of people hated Dave, and nobody enjoyed working on his team. If Dave was Marcie's idea of a leader, I didn't blame her one bit for not wanting to be one. I didn't want to be anything like Dave, either.

I asked Marcie if she could think of any leaders in the company who were different from Dave. I named some specific men and women who practiced a much more collegial style. Marcie agreed they were effective leaders.

I also pointed out that Marcie was already performing several critical leadership functions such as teaching, encouragement, and leading by example. She was surprised to hear this, and admitted that she didn't really think of those things as a key part of a leader's job.

I asked Marcie if she had ever heard me raise my voice to a member of our team. She said no, never.

And what about Jane, I asked (the leader of another team in our office)? Had Marcie ever heard of Jane dressing down a team member in front of all her colleagues?

Again, Marcie said no.

"Well, then," I said, "is it possible there is more than one way to be a leader?"

Marcie agreed there was.

"Could you see yourself being a leader more like Jane, or Bill, or maybe even like me?"

Marcie smiled. "Well…maybe," she said.

I told Marcie that I believed she was ready to get on the leadership track that could lead to promotion. I asked her to think about it for a few days before making a final decision. Over the rest of that week, we had several more discussions about leadership and what makes a good leader. We talked about the different styles of leadership. I promised Marcie that if she agreed to begin leadership training, and that once she was promoted I would be available to help her in any way I could, if she ever ran into a situation that made her uncomfortable.

At the end of the week, Marcie agreed to get on the leadership track. I'm delighted to say that she was subsequently promoted to leader status and quickly became one of the most successful executives in our region. Marcie led with encouragement and support, not criticism and negativity. Her team consistently turned in one of the highest performance records in our company.

Not surprisingly, Marcie was extremely popular with her team, too. She never bossed people around, never yelled at people, and never humiliated them. She simply capitalized on what she was already doing informally with one person at a time, making constructive suggestions and employing a teaching approach. As a leader, she expanded this approach to several people at a time.

As the next several years rolled by, Marcie rose through the ranks of our company, eventually taking my position when I moved up, and later succeeding Bill at the national level when he retired.

Marcie -- who began by hating the whole idea of being a "leader" – turned out to be one of the most successful leaders I've ever known. A woman who was convinced that she didn't have what it takes, proved that she had every gift required for successful leadership – as long as she could define leadership on her own terms.

(Before we continue, let me say that the "reluctant leader" phenomenon is not confined solely to women. Men have it, too. A famous example is Audie Murphy, winner of the Congressional Medal of Honor and the most decorated combat soldier in U.S. history. While serving as an Army infantryman in World War Two, Murphy repeatedly turned down promotions. He did so despite the fact that – as his commanding officers pointed out – he naturally assumed responsibility and repeatedly took actions to lead and protect his fellow soldiers in the field. Despite his obvious leadership skills, Murphy just didn't see himself as "officer material.")

Stories like Marcie's, and examples like Audie Murphy, raise a very important question. What exactly _is_ leadership?

There are dozens of leadership models... and many of them seem to cancel each other out!

This is where the mystery of leadership comes in. One of the reasons for the confusion over this issue is that there are so many plausible-sounding answers. An astonishing variety of models and definitions of leadership have been touted over the years, many supported by reams of studies and objective" data. Yet many of these leadership theories have little or nothing in common with each other. Some models of leadership even flatly contradict each other. For example...

The Persuasion Model:

Is leadership the *ability to persuade* others to voluntarily support your platform, as a gifted leader must do to lead a successful movement or a popularly elected government? To be a good leader, do you have to demonstrate the eloquence of a Franklin Roosevelt or an Abraham Lincoln?

The Incentive Model:

Is leadership the skill of *setting the right goals and creating the right incentives* to motivate high performance, as we see in corporate posts from CEO to Executive Sales Director? Are the ideal leaders people who focus on rewarding excellence, like Tonda Ferguson, Southwest Airlines' senior director of employee engagement, or Rymax Marketing President and COO Eve Kolakowski?

The Inspiration Model:

Is leadership about setting a tone of zealous dedication and *creating the unconquerable desire to win*, as in top-level pro athletic coaching? Does true leadership mean emulating winners like Green Bay Packers legend Vince Lombardi or today's DeLisha Milton-Jones, the two-time Olympic gold medalist who became head coach at Pepperdine University, and then at Old Dominion University?

The Nurturing Model:

Is leadership about *quietly nurturing your team* with a caregiving model, or playing a "hidden hand" or "facilitator" role, so that your team members know you have their backs, and they feel empowered to go out and be great at their jobs? Is the best type of leader a shy introvert like my former colleague Marcie -- or perhaps a soft-spoken person like Nelson Mandela, who famously said: "Lead from the back, and let others think they are in front."

The Conquest Model:

Or, is leadership a matter of having *a loud voice and a tough image*, projecting fearlessness, and communicating the will and know-how to successfully fight the battle against all odds? To be an effective leader, do you have to have a commanding, overbearing personality like General George S. Patton, or Steve Jobs?

These are just a few of the many competing models and definitions of leadership that circulate through today's world. Each has its zealous advocates and successful examples.

Which model of leadership is the best? Which theory is the correct one? *What is true leadership?*

My own definition: leadership is about influence

I find it useful to take the broadest possible view of the question. As I see it, a leader is *anyone who influences the thoughts and behaviors of themselves or others*.

Again, leadership begins with self-leadership. When you change your thinking in order to manage your emotions and ultimately impact your own actions, you're exercising a form of self-influence – and that is leadership.

Leadership in the broadest sense also includes being a role model whose example or inspiration has an impact on others – even if the role model never meets the follower or knows they exist. This is true, for example, of sports figures who are admired by millions of kids who want to emulate them. It's true of social media influencers who have 20 million followers whose ideas and lifestyles are influenced by their idols. It's also true of admired figures in a family or in a small community, whom others look up to and want to please or earn the respect of. These are leaders in our society and their influence is a form of leadership.

When we look at the more formal, traditional types of leadership where there is someone with authority, a group of followers, and a mutual goal for the team to pursue, influence is exercised in a more conscious and deliberate way – but influence is still at the heart of leadership.

Great leadership can embrace dozens of different styles and models, depending on the institutional environment, the occasion or situation, the nature of the challenge, the talents and skills of the leader, and the range of roles and personalities involved. Regardless of whether we're talking about a business, a social club, a community organization like the PTA or the Scouts, a sports team, a government organization, the Armed Forces, or any other setting, being a *good* leader or an *effective* leader involves the art and science of setting the right goals, having the right values for that particular post and community, setting the right example, and knowing when, where and how to practice the appropriate leadership styles and techniques.

There are times and places when the winning strategy is to be General Patton. There are other situations where the right model to emulate is Mother Teresa. There are challenges that call for the compassion- ate skills and faith-based talents of a Martin Luther King, Jr., and there are other environments that demand the technocratic gifts of a Sheryl Sandberg.

There are forms of leadership that mostly demand embodying and defending the rules and traditions (for example, Chief Justice of the Supreme Court). At the same time, in very different arenas, there are forms of leadership that require pioneering and rule-breaking (avant-garde artist or disruptive innovator).

So, if there are many different, many "right" styles of leadership, depending on the circumstances -- and if there are three core ele- ments common to all leadership -- that leaves us facing the ultimate bottom-line question, and the most perplexing mystery about the whole subject.

Are leaders born or made?

Here is where the mythology of leadership comes strongly to the fore. When it comes to this question, our society tends to be of two minds.

On the one hand, it certainly appears that many of us strongly believe leadership involves skills that can be taught, and concepts that can be learned. Otherwise, why would we read and write books, and take or teach workshops, on the subject? Why else would there be "schools of leadership" and "Leadership Certification Training" all over the place?

Yet simultaneously, at some deep level, many people seem to feel that leadership is a magical, even mystical, quality. You either have it or you don't. We may describe one person as a "born leader," or speak admiringly of another person's "charismatic" leadership style.

I don't know about you, but I haven't seen too many successful Schools of Charisma around. If you think leadership is charisma, you probably feel that it can't be taught, and perhaps I would even agree with that.

Some people go farther than just suggesting leadership is inborn. They flatly deny that leadership can be successfully taught in any way whatsoever. Here's one example from an opinion piece published a few years ago in *Forbes* magazine:

"I don't believe leadership can be taught, it's either a part of your DNA or it isn't. The ability to show empathy, engage, empower, and inspire others is just not something that can be trained into someone."[2]

I find myself in 100% disagreement with this statement. I don't believe anyone arrives on Planet Earth with an inborn knowledge of how to exercise authority and meet responsibility, set the right goals, and attract or manage followers.

In addition, I believe anyone who says, "I am not a leader" is saying they have zero percent control over themselves, and over what they think and do. I believe we are all leaders. Again, we are leaders of ourselves first, and then we can become leaders of others if we decide to be.

Most of all, I am totally, passionately convinced that leadership can be learned by those who are open-minded and willing to work at learning it. In fact, I am quite certain that effective leadership is based on a set

---

2   Joe Morgan, "Why You Can't Teach Leadership," *Forbes,* Aug. 26, 2015; https://www.forbes.com/sites/jacobmorgan/2015/08/26/why-you-cant-teach-leadership/#6b9e853f2c99

of skills that tens of thousands of people are successfully acquiring and perfecting, every day.

Here is the most important fact that I know to be the absolute, fundamental truth about leadership:

Leadership is a journey to follow, not an inborn talent to exercise. And it's certainly not a pose to strike!

How do I know this is true?

Because I myself have taken the journey from frightened follower to confident leader. What's more, I have introduced thousands of other people to the path they can follow to career success and personal fulfilment through skillful, effective leadership.

I know for sure that leadership can be learned, because I have acquired my own leadership skills after starting my corporate career with zero leadership knowledge or ability.

Me, a born leader? Ha! I was about as far from it as you can get. As the story of my panic attacks shows, fairly early in my career I *failed spectacularly* -- in an episode of my life that is still painful for me to think about.

But I refused to accept my failure as my fate. I looked at failure and ignorance as problems to be solved, not a curse that would inevitably hang over the rest of my life and would ruin my entire future.

Instead of saying, *"Well, I'm doomed. Leaders are born, not made, and I am obviously not one of them"* -- I did just the opposite.

I picked myself up, dusted myself off, and began traveling the road from failure to success. Eventually, I made the journey from hapless non-leader to a person with effective, proven leadership skills.

Millions of others have done the same thing, or traveled much tougher roads than I did. Back in 1996 J.K. Rowling was living in poverty as a single mother on welfare, but she believed in herself and became the world's bestselling children's book author. (By the way, her first Harry Potter novel was rejected by many publishers – but she stuck with it. Now she is a leader to millions through the influence of her books, among other things.)

How long does it take to go from "zero to hero" and learn leadership skills? That depends on you. But I know this much: the journey to better leadership never ends – and *you don't want it to end* -- because this is a skill that you can always learn more about and improve on.

Over the course of my own journey, I kept learning, kept growing, and kept trying until I reached the level where today – 16 years after my humiliating early failure -- I not only have a long track record of successful leadership (and the career and financial rewards that go with it); I also have the joy and reward of sharing what I've learned with others.

How else do I know that leadership can be learned?

Because every single day, my clients tell me that they are putting these lessons into practice. Hour by hour, step by step, job by job, they are becoming ever more confident and successful.

They are seeing the impact of their influence on the world around them. They are getting rewarded with money and position. They are experiencing the joys of teamwork when everything is humming like a well-oiled machine, and when others look to them for guidance and vision.

They are becoming *leaders.*

How do you begin the journey to leadership?

If leadership is a skill that can be learned, how do you go about learning it? If leadership is a road rather than a destination, how do you get started on a successful journey?

How do you rebound from "panic attack victim" to confident, professional financial leader and globe-hopping public speaker? On a far larger scale, how to you rise from fired local TV anchor to beloved global media mogul?

One step at a time, that's how.

The journey to successful leadership is, in the classic phrase, "a game of inches." Our next milestone on the path, and our next chapter, will reveal how a series of small gains – steps so small, they barely seem worth taking – can accumulate and grow into gigantic leaps forward.

CHAPTER 3

The path to becoming a leader, one step at a time

Like any task, leadership is easier if you divide it into small, manageable steps. Eventually they add up to something big!

Question: What links Mother Teresa's famous hospice in Calcutta and an Olympic Gold Medal-winning bicycle team in Europe?

What could these two organizations, separated by thousands of miles and dedicated to totally different missions, possibly have common?

Answer: Both organizations achieved world-class impact in part because their leaders adopted a strategy of *incrementalism,* which is the technique of achieving a goal by moving forward in small steps.

British Cycling: from zeroes to heroes

Bicycle racing fans are probably familiar with the amazing transformation of British Cycling, the UK's national governing organization for the sport. In the early 2000s, BC took its teams from among the worst-performing in international sports to some of the best in their field.

British Cycling had plenty of room for improvement when they got started. Their humiliating track record included just one Olympic Gold Medal from 1908 to 2003. What's more, British cyclists had *never* taken home the trophy for the Tour de France. Not once!

Part of the problem was money. They just didn't have the funding to hire the people they needed to turn the organization around. That changed in the 1990s when the UK National Lottery began contributing significant sums to BC's budget.

They spent the money well, hiring advanced coaches and sports psychologists, and starting to design their own equipment.

In 2003, BC promoted its programs director David Brailsford to the post of Performance Director. Brailsford had been a cycling fanatic (he calls himself "tenacious") since age 18, when he left home, traveled from the UK to a small town in France and talked himself into a spot on a French racing team. In the evenings, bored with no friends and no ability to speak French, he began to read everything he could find on the emerging fields of sports psychology and sports science. He became so intrigued by these subjects that he returned to Britain and studied them at the university.

From these experiences and lessons, Brailsford came up with his game-changing approach, which he calls "the accumulation of marginal gains." Basically, it means taking a lot of baby steps that combine to produce a transformational effect. As Brailsford himself puts it:

"The whole principle came from the idea that if you broke down everything you could think of that goes into riding a bike, and then improved [each function and component] by 1%, you will get a significant increase when you put them all together."[3]

Applying the philosophy, and earning a series of victories

Some of the changes that BC promoted were so tiny that you might wonder how they could possibly make a significant difference. Some of the changes included:

- They designed more comfortable bike seats.

---

3   Slater, Matt (8 August 2012). "Olympics cycling: Marginal gains underpin Team GB dominance". BBC Sport. Retrieved 11 April 2014.

- They coated bicycle tires with alcohol for better road traction.
- After wind tunnel tests showed indoor cycling suits were more aerodynamic, BC had outdoor riders wear them, too.
- They painted the inside of their transport truck with white paint so dust showed up more easily, making it easier to keep the truck interior spotlessly clean – thus keeping the bikes free of dust that could impede performance by infinitesimal amounts.[4]

These were just some of the hundreds of improvements that BC adopted for its bikes and riders, from better handwashing technique (less chance of getting a cold) to better massage gels (faster recovery from muscle injury).

In 2008, British Cycling walked off – or rode off – with 60% of the gold medals available in their sport at the Beijing Olympics. They did even better at the 2012 Olympics. They also won a string of Tour de France victories from 2012 to 2017.

This should not come as a surprise! "The accumulation of marginal gains" is based on commonsense principles

What explains this dramatic turnaround? Did BC suddenly recruit a new generation of super-athletes who effortlessly achieved natural dominance over their sport?

Not at all. They simply leveraged three simple principles that every schoolchild is familiar with.

Principle #1: "Slow and steady wins the race" – especially slow and steady efforts to get a little bit better, day by day, over the long haul.

Principle #2: "You have to put your pants on one leg at a time." Nearly every task, every mission, and every goal requires us to perform a series of small, intermediate steps. Another way of expressing the same idea is the well-known statement from Chinese philosopher Lao Tzu: "A journey of a thousand miles begins with a single step."

---

4   Clear, James, *Atomic Habits*: Excerpted at https://jamesclear.com/marginal-gains.

Principle #3: "Small things make a big difference." You can accumulate far more wealth by starting with a penny and doubling it every day, as opposed to receiving a check for $1 million on Day 1 and just sitting on it for a month. With the penny doubling daily, you end up with more than $5 million.

Math teachers and bankers call this "the power of compound interest." But it's also an illustration of why incrementalism works in leadership. David Brailsford and his colleagues never asked their athletes to do the impossible, or to make insane leaps of progress overnight. They merely urged their cyclists and support teams to focus on small, achievable steps – and stick with it.

Mother Teresa: saving humanity, one person at a time

Practicing leadership in small steps works for everyone, in every field.

Five thousand miles from British Cycling's UK headquarters -- and a world away in terms of culture – the nun we know today as Mother Teresa founded her Missionaries of Charity organization in Calcutta. She began with a school, then a social support services initiative to support "the poorest of the poor."

She added a hospice to care for people in the last stages of life, providing medical care and enabling them to die with dignity in the tradition of their faith, whether they were Christians, Hindus or Muslims. But she didn't stop there. Next came a shelter for homeless children, more hospices, orphanages, and leper houses across India. After 15 years of success in India, she expanded her movement abroad to dozens of missions, hospitals, schools, orphanages and shelters around the world – including Asia, Africa, Europe and the U.S.

For her amazing work, Mother Teresa eventually won the Nobel Peace Prize and was beatified by the Catholic Church as a saint.

This was the journey of a leader who began with no food, no home, and no financial support, walking the dusty roads of India exhausted and in pain, just looking for a place to sleep.

Obviously, Mother Teresa's astonishing success is a prime example of "one step at a time leadership" in action. Her decades-long progression from leading a single school to heading a global network of social and medical service organizations could probably not have been accomplished any other way.

But "one step at a time" was more than just a strategy for Mother Teresa. It was the reflection of a deeply held philosophy and belief system.

The philosophy is expressed in the most famous statement she ever made: "Not all of us can do great things. But we can do small things with great love."

The belief system was revealed after her death to a group of managers who came to Mother Teresa's headquarters in Calcutta, seeking to learn her leadership secrets. The visitors asked if Mother Teresa had "set any big, audacious goals, like eliminating poverty."

Sister Prema, Superior General of the Missionaries of Charity, replied: "Oh, no. Mother Teresa was completely focused on helping one person at a time."[5]

What if you prefer disruptive innovation and big, bold initiatives?

Whenever the subject of incrementalism comes up, there are always people who object:

"That's fine for some people, but I'm not interested in gradual, incremental improvements. The situation demands large-scale, sweeping, transformational change – right now! We must achieve a massive transformation as soon as possible."

---

5   https://govleaders.org/one-person-at-a-time.htm

The desire for overnight transformation is exciting, to be sure, and there are situations where it is absolutely the best move for leaders to call for such audacious goals.

At the same time, it's a misunderstanding to assume that adopting massive, rapid change as your goal means there is no place for the "small steps" approach. It's not either/or. We need both. In fact, the bigger the ultimate goal, the more important it is to break it down into steps.

Learning from NASA and the first Moon mission

Let's look at what many people regard as the most audacious goal of the 20th century: putting an astronaut on the Moon.

When President Kennedy announced this mission in 1961, he certainly didn't talk about small steps or incremental change. He said, "I believe that this nation should commit itself to achieving the goal, before this decade is out, of landing a man on the Moon and returning him safely to Earth."

As has been said, you can't leap a chasm in two leaps! President Kennedy understood this, and that's why he set the bar high. He also knew that adopting such an ambitious goal would have a rallying effect and would inspire the entire nation to put forth its best efforts.

At the same time, NASA was the organization charged with carrying out the Moon mission. NASA did not throw a team of astronauts on top of a rocket the day after Kennedy's speech and say, "Good luck, guys, we haven't updated our hardware for this new mission, and we haven't tested this rocket very much, but we're sending you to the Moon anyway – we hope – because we really need overnight, transformational change."

Instead, NASA spent years on a careful, step-by-step program to develop and perfect the technology, control systems, astronaut skills and spaceflight strategies that could turn Kennedy's vision into a reality in a safe, reliable way.

- The Apollo 4 and 6 missions were unmanned exercises to test design elements and certify safety.

- The Apollo 7 mission was a manned test of the combined rocket and Command Service Module in Earth orbit.

- Apollo 8 tested the complete Command Module and Lunar Module together in Earth orbit for the first time, and then its crew of three astronauts flew off to orbit the Moon.

- The crew of Apollo 10 performed final testing in lunar orbit, without landing.

- Apollo 11 finally made the first human landing on the Moon.

This combination of Kennedy's audacious, overriding goal with NASA's careful, step-by-step execution, provides fresh insight into the first words ever spoken on the lunar surface: "That's one small step for a man, one giant leap for mankind."

Simply put, the first Moon landing was <u>both</u> a disruptive leap forward, and also a result of gradual, incremental steps. Perhaps that was part of the point that Neil Armstrong was making!

To learn leadership skills on a step-by-step basis, you need these 2 emotional strengths

Learning to be a leader is like taking the British Cycling team from perpetual losers to perpetual winners. It is an ambitious goal but the best way to tackle it is with an incremental, step-by-step approach. Even if the art of leadership feels completely foreign to us, if we take it one step at a time, we can eventually become very skilled at it.

The great thing is, you can start making a (small) difference immediately, and keep making more and more of a difference next week, next month, next year – forever.

But the step-by-step approach takes two emotional strengths that are sometimes hard to come by: commitment and patience. (Don't believe me? Just ask anyone who has ever gone on a diet.)

First, we must commit to our goal. We must promise ourselves that we are going to make this goal important in our lives. We are going to work hard and stick with it. We must get clear about the need to invest a certain amount of time and effort, and we must recognize the need to be consistent in applying ourselves.

Next, we must be patient in waiting for results. We must accept the fact that the rewards of incremental learning will not come over-night. When the British Cycling organization began making their 1% changes, nothing appeared to make much difference at first. Why should it? It's only a 1% change! Most people can't detect a 1% dif-ference in anything. (Could you look at a jar of 100 pennies and a jar of 101 pennies, and tell them apart? I couldn't.)

But over time, all those 1% changes, all those small steps, all that com-mitment to ongoing effort, achieves a "compound interest" effect.

The question is, how do we *maintain our commitment* while we wait for that effect to show up? How do we *remain patient* as we keep working for our goal, without seeing large, immediate results?

One part of the answer can be found on a bamboo farm.

Why bamboo farmers can be learning success models

Bamboo is a plant (technically, a type of grass) with some remarkable properties. Of its many species, some varieties can be planted and don't produce much visible growth for two or three years, but then they start growing 10 feet per month. Some species remain a lowly bush for the first couple of years, then shoot up to a 130-foot tall group of canes in years three, four or five (in the right climate, with the right care).

How does this happen? During the first few years, most of the growth is taking place in the underground root system. You can't see it but the farmer knows it's there, and he knows that if he keeps nurturing the plant, it will eventually yield an impressive harvest. What's more, it will seem like an almost overnight success story — certainly compared to growing an oak tree, which can take more than a century to reach full maturity!

The lesson of the successful bamboo farmer is not that "if you keep doing the same thing over and over without getting any results, eventually your efforts will pay off regardless." It depends entirely on whether you are pursuing a winning strategy in a promising environment, and properly executing that strategy. But assuming that you meet all those tests, there are definitely times when knowing that a positive outcome is virtually guaranteed, can help us achieve long-term perspective, which contributes mightily to patience.

At the same time, it also helps if you can get positive feedback every step of the way. Human beings live for feedback, the more immediate the better. How can we get encouraging feedback on a regular basis that helps us be patient as we executive a long-term, incremental, step-by-step strategy?

Introducing the Competency Ladder

I have found that one of the most effective conceptual frameworks that helps us remain committed and keep our patience as we learn the art of leadership (or work toward any long-term learning goal), is a matrix known as the Competency Ladder, or the "four stages of confidence."

The Competency Ladder is an ascending pyramid that illustrates how we all go through 4 basic stages, whenever we learn a new skill. (This extremely useful tool was invented and refined in the late 1960s and the 1970s by management trainers and life coaches including Martin Broadwell, Paul Curtis and Phillip Warren, and Noel Burch.)

Stage 1: "Unconscious incompetence."

This is when we don't know anything about the skill, and we're not even aware of how ignorant we truly are.

For example, suppose you decide to learn to scuba dive. Before your first lesson, you will probably know nothing about clearing your mask, regulating your tanks, and performing pre-dive checks.

In addition, you may never have heard of breathing from a "demand valve," exercising buoyancy control, maintaining trim, and using the signal system for communicating underwater. You don't even know that you are missing all of this vital information!

But in this stage, the learner may be full of excitement and enthusiasm. They don't realize they have a long road ahead of them, and that it will be full of failures and setbacks – or at least, hard work to acquire certain core competencies. All they can see is the reward, how much fun it's going to be to swim underwater and explore the ocean.

Stage 2: "Conscious incompetence."

In this phase, we advance to the next rung on the ladder (or move up to the next level of the pyramid) and become aware of the lessons that we have to learn – but we're often not any good at performing the required tasks.

Yes, we know now that we have to breathe through the demand valve, but we may not have the hang of it yet. The same goes for all the other skills on the list.

At this point, the enthusiastic beginner often becomes a "disillusioned learner." They may say, "I'll never master all this material. I'll never gain all these skills. It's too hard. Maybe I should quit." (For an example closer to home, just ask somebody who is just starting to learn to play golf).

But if the learner stays with it, and has a good teacher, and a modest amount of aptitude, they can almost always learn from their mistakes. Every disappointing result becomes another lesson, and another opportunity to learn a valuable skill or principle.

Stage 3: "Conscious competence."

This is the stage where we are technically able do everything required to perform our tasks, but we have to think about it and keep our minds focused sharply on each step or each action as we perform it. The name of the game here is *concentration*, and the performance of our newly acquired skills may feel mechanical and unnatural.

In Stage 3, the learner can veer back and forth from excited overconfidence – "Look, ma, I'm scuba diving!" – to nervous apprehension: "Wait, did I set the tanks properly? Am I keeping in trim? How's my valve breathing? Whoops, is my mask starting to fog up? Am I properly equalizing the pressure as I ascend to the surface, so I don't hurt my ears or my lungs? Gosh, there are so many things to pay attention to! This is scary!"

Stage 4: "Unconscious competence."

In the final and uppermost stage of the pyramid, the learner has performed the skills correctly so many times that they become second nature. The learner is now a skilled actor, on their way to becoming an expert. They can swing that golf club, ride that bicycle, fly that airplane, or be a skillful and safe diver, without having to think about what they're doing in such an obsessive way.

Emotionally, when you reach Stage 4 you can afford to relax and enjoy the ride a little bit. If you're now a certified scuba diver, you can appreciate the view of the marine life. If you're a team leader, you can begin to have fun dealing with the people you're leading.

You may also feel a new sense of excitement and empowerment: "Hey, I can really do this! And, I can get even better at it! There is no stopping me now, and no telling how far I can go!"

Knowing about the Competency Ladder gives us one way to mentally gauge our progress as we get started learning leadership skills, step by step. Putting things into an expected context, helps us acquire patience.

For example, when you hit the "disillusioned learner" phase, it helps to realize: "Hey, everybody goes through this. It's normal to feel a bit discouraged or overwhelmed at first. And, it's not permanent."

More support for the journey of leadership: the importance of mentors

This is where a good mentor comes in. In fact, mentors are invaluable at every stage of the Competency Ladder.

When we are Unconsciously Incompetent, a mentor can teach us the basics of the skills that we need to learn.

When we become Consciously Incompetent, a mentor can not only provide focused lessons to get us over the rough spots; they can also provide encouragement and praise when we get something right – and even more, when we get something wrong. Again, humans thrive on positive feedback.

In the Conscious Competence phase, a good mentor can provide feedback that allows us to fine-tune our skills. The mentor may also show us how to put all of our newly learned skills together into an integrated package. And, a good mentor will caution us against premature confidence or overconfidence, and will calm us when we feel overwhelmed by all the lessons that we have to keep in mind.

In the Unconscious Competence phase, a good mentor can help you get deeper lessons from what you are doing right. For example, the mentor might prod you to think through why a particular action or tactic succeeded, so you can apply it even more effectively next time. And, your mentor can help you start to integrate everything you've learned into the other areas of your work, or your life.

Congratulations. You have taken the first step on the step-by-step path to leadership!

I like the Competency Ladder because it gives us a "mental architecture" for the step-by-step approach to learning to be a leader (or learn any skill, for that matter). This mental framework is invaluable, because if you're going on a journey, you need a map. The Competency Ladder is an important part of your map.

Like everything in life, when it comes to learning leadership skills, attitude is 90% of success. Most of us have forgotten the learning approach that we used in the first years of life, when our brains were self-organizing, and we were learning new things at an exponential rate.

As countless parents have observed, when a child begins learning to walk, they fall down — a lot. But they don't hit themselves on the head and say, "Bad! Failure! Awful!" Instead, they cheerfully get up and toddle another couple of steps, until they fall down again and start the process over.

Gradually, they learn to keep their balance, learn the "controlled fall" that is walking. They learn to put one foot in front of the other, to shift their weight and stay on their feet.

And quite often, they are just as delighted with their failures as with their successes. Very young children seem to instinctively realize that falling down or failing in some other way, is all part of the learning process. It's a necessary component of exploring what it is to be alive.

When we say that creative minds are those that maintain a "child-like attitude" into adulthood, this is a huge part of what we mean. *Children don't realize they're working at learning to walk. For them, it's a form of play.* They sense they can do it, they see their parents walking, and they want to do the same.

Most of your growth as a leader will be during your greatest challenges. Yes, you will fall down! And, in the early phases of learning leadership, you frequently will not see quick results. You will second-guess yourself. You will feel like abandoning the whole enterprise.

If you ever feel this way, I have a message for you. Keep going! Trust the process. Embrace the journey. You have taken the crucial first step, and that is something to celebrate. Eventually, if you're in the right field, and especially if you have a good mentor, your bamboo will grow. Your natural talents will merge with your freshly acquired skills.

And you'll be one day closer to being Tomorrow's Leader.

CHAPTER 4

To begin your journey to leadership, start by "clearing the path."

There are 10 common blind spots that can prevent you becoming a successful leader. Fortunately, they're all curable.

I want to share two quick stories about two very different leaders, both newly promoted to the job. The first leader quickly proved to be a surprising failure, for reasons that nobody saw coming.

The second leader turned out to be a huge, almost shocking success, whose hidden strengths became increasingly obvious as time went on.

Both stories are true. For now, we'll call the first leader "Eric" and the second leader "Louis." (We'll discuss their real identities a bit later).

When Eric took command, everyone expected great things

Eric was a financial advisor at the nationwide firm I worked for. Eric not only led our regional office in sales; for five straight years, he led the entire national organization. His performance was miles ahead of everyone else's.

Eric's achievements were built on a brilliant mind and incredible communication skills. He also conveyed overwhelming self-confidence; he almost swaggered. All these factors combined to give Eric a tremendous aura of success. Everyone in our company wanted to work with him and learn from him. Whenever Eric gave a workshop, we all wrote down every word he said.

In our company, anyone who delivered that kind of performance was expected to step up and take on leadership responsibilities. When Eric finally made this move, we all said, "This guy is going to make an unbelievably successful leader."

He ended up failing miserably. Eric assumed everybody else just naturally thought and learned the way he did, and that everyone on his team started from the same motives, goals and perspectives that were identical to his. Whenever one of Eric's team members had trouble learning a concept or technique, he became frustrated, even angry at people who didn't see his point of view. He insisted they must think like him, speak like him, and almost become "Eric clones."

If one of his team was unable to make a presentation or close a sale the way Eric felt that he could, he would criticize that team member harshly. He did not offer constructive criticism or gentle suggestions; he almost insulted his subordinates. Finally, rather than supporting people on his team who needed help, and instead of giving them additional training and development, Eric stopped communicating with them. He *abandoned* them.

In a short time, company members went from admiring Eric to avoiding him. He threw away all the trust, respect and admiration that he'd built up over five years. Ultimately Eric left the company.

Eric turned out to be a textbook case of "how not to lead a team."

When Louis got the top job, many people feared the worst

Almost the opposite story occurred with a leader we'll call "Louis."

Louis had been a compromise choice as executive vice-president. The organization had a rigid, locked-in leadership structure, so when the CEO departed, Louis was automatically promoted to the top job, at least temporarily.

From Day One, negative rumors began to circulate about Louis, and there were widespread predictions of his failure. People whispered that he wasn't up to the job. He had a mousy, quiet personality, totally unlike the dynamic, charismatic CEO he was replacing. Louis came from a small-town background and had never even attended college. Worst of all, there were vague rumors of a brush with organized crime somewhere in his past.

How could this unpromising figure inspire confidence? How could he hope to be anything more than a temporary caretaker in the top job?

Louis immediately defied all the negative expectations. He built a strong leadership team around himself, because he wasn't afraid of being "outshone" by people with more dazzling styles or better reputations.

What's more, Louis turned out to be a tough, decisive leader who made great judgment calls in a crisis. When he felt deeply that a certain policy was right, he had the courage to push it through, even if nobody else liked his decision. He nearly always proved to be right.

When it came time to select a new CEO on a long-term basis, Louis got the job.

Leadership isn't about the aura you create; it's about the judgment calls you make

As mentioned, both of these are true stories. Eric worked with me at Ameriprise, the financial services company. Perhaps Eric could have stayed at the company if he'd gone back to being a financial advisor, but he wasn't interested. He'd gotten a taste of the prestige of leadership, and he was determined to show the world that he could succeed at it.

Over the next several years, Eric moved through several companies and failed at a series of leadership posts. His life eventually went into a tailspin. For obvious reasons, I don't want to give his real name.

The story of "Louis" is actually the story of Harry S. Truman, a compromise choice for Vice President who became the 33rd President of the United States.

At first Truman's quiet, undemonstrative personality compared poorly with that of his flamboyant predecessor, Franklin Roosevelt. Truman's critics claimed he owed his start in politics to a crooked political machine back in his home state of Missouri.

But as President, Truman built a great team — including giants like George Marshall, Dean Acheson, and Clark Clifford — and he made great decisions, from establishing NATO to launching the Marshall Plan, inventing the "containment strategy" to keep the Cold War under control, and desegregating the U.S. military.

Much of what made President Truman a great leader was the opposite of what made "Eric" a failed leader. Where Eric was arrogant, rigid and insisted that everyone on his team must think and act exactly like him, Truman was humble, surrounded himself with staff of diverse backgrounds, and valued the differences between himself and others. He did his best to learn from those with more experience.

Where Eric expected his team to make him look good, Truman never forgot that he was there to serve the public interest, even if it cost him short-term popularity.

Eric was skilled at creating the aura of success, but that aura only took him so far. Truman was focused on what counted -- meeting his larger responsibilities and getting solid results. That ethic took him from small beginnings to an honored place in the history books.

Self-leadership has its roots in self-awareness, which can reveal the 10 most common obstacles to success

If you want to become a successful leader, the best place to begin is by understanding what makes for leadership effectiveness, and what holds people back from succeeding.

I have repeatedly seen 10 common obstacles that block leaders from achieving success, even those like Eric who have great potential. These common obstacles are:

1) Egotism: thinking you have all the answers, and unwillingness to learn from others (especially those you perceive as less successful or less important).

2) The "natural leader" myth: believing that leaders have inborn traits that cannot be acquired or learned.

3) The "omni-expert" myth: assuming that a leader must have superior skills or knowledge on every relevant topic, compared to those led.

4) Laziness or rigidness: failure to study leadership and learn from great leaders.

5) Narrowmindedness: valuing teammates because they think like you do, or because they come from similar backgrounds.

6) The "mirror syndrome": assuming everyone is "like me" in how they think, approach problems, communicate, perceive things, etc.

7) Overvaluing peace and harmony: a desire to avoid confrontation and conflict at all costs.

8) Desire to be liked: taking actions based on what others will think, instead of doing or saying what needs to be done.

9) <u>Worshipping consensus</u> as an end in itself: making it your goal to get everyone to agree on a goal or policy, first and foremost.

10) <u>Lack of authenticity</u>: putting on a false front or pretending to be someone they are not, leading to a breakdown in trust.

A searching, honest self-appraisal is the first requirement of successful leadership. If you identify any of these roadblocks or blind spots in yourself, or think you do, it's time to practice self-leadership and take steps to correct or overcome them. Then and only then can you be successful and effective at leading others.

Let's briefly look at these 10 roadblocks, one at a time.

Obstacle #1: Egotism

Many would-be leaders ask, "What's wrong with having a strong ego? Isn't that what makes someone want to be a leader in the first place?"

That's true as far as it goes. But having a healthy self-regard is one thing; having a closed mind or contempt for others is quite another matter. Successful leadership requires checking your ego at the door, in the sense of getting over your sense of self-importance or superiority.

You can learn from anyone, and a good leader tries to learn from everyone.

I once knew a very successful leader in our financial services company named Paul. After three years in his post, he had become one the best performers at this level in the country.

But Paul fell short in one area: he wasn't very good at getting his team members to pass the financial services exam. I suggested he pick up the phone and talk to Kim, a leader in a similar position on the other side of the country. Kim was nowhere near as effective as Paul in building a great sales organization, but she was knocking it out of the park when it came to helping her people pass the all-important financial services test.

When I suggested that Paul talk to her, he said: "You've got to be kidding. She's number 98 on the company scorecard; why should I listen to her?"

Finally, I talked Paul into asking Kim how she managed to get so many of her people to pass those exams. He spent an hour on the phone with her, and quickly realized she knew a lot of valuable lessons he didn't have a clue about. He put his ego aside and applied Kim's philosophy to his own team. Before you know it, Paul's team members were also passing the financial services exam with flying colors.

Today Paul freely admits that he was too egotistical and that he learned far more from this situation than simply how to coach exam takers. He learned a crucial lesson in the value of humility.

A successful leader is humble enough to understand that you've got people in your organization who can and will contribute in a huge way to the team's success – if you invite them to do so. It's part of the leader's job to open the door to that participation so that everyone feels welcome to provide feedback and ideas, and to express their views.

If you fail to do that, you are throwing away valuable company assets. But if you make it your practice to solicit those contributions, you not only leverage the company's knowledge base (and build your own knowledge); you also earn the respect and loyalty of your colleagues and team members.

Obstacles #2 and #3: The "natural leader" myth and the "omni-expert" myth

The myths of the "natural leader" and the "omni-expert" are based on the mistaken beliefs that a leader is born, not made; that a leader must have a larger-than-life personality, brimming with style and charisma; and that that a leader must always know more than everyone on his or her team on every topic that involves the company's business.

We touched on these myths, without naming them as such, in the story of Marcie, back in Chapter Two. The story of Harry Truman is another great example. Here, let me simply point to the fact that President Truman never apologized for his quiet, plain-vanilla style, but he did make sure to tell the truth. Likewise, Truman never apologized for what he didn't know, but he did consult earnestly with experts, and he read stacks of briefing papers from his staff every night, to make sure he was up to speed on all the crucial decisions he had to make.

Whenever I think about introverts who made great leaders, I remember Patriots football coach Bill Belichick, a low-key personality yet an incredibly successful leader. I also think of a CEO named Jim that I used to work with. He was so shy, introverted and soft-spoken that having a conversation with him could be almost painful. His extreme discomfort made those he spoke with feel uncomfortable, too.

Despite this drawback, Jim was smart, sincere, respectful, thoughtful, fair, and exercised good judgment – which made him a great leader.

The truth about leadership is, no one is born a leader, and no one can be the ultimate expert on every relevant topic. But with or without a big personality, most people can become effective leaders if they work at it, and most leaders can make a strength – not a liability – of surrounding themselves with experts who know more than they do.

Obstacle #4: Laziness or rigidness

Paul had a deficiency in his leadership style, partly because he wasn't interested in learning from people he perceived as less successful. But there are some who refuse to learn, even from the most successful leaders in every field.

Clearly, readers of this book don't have this problem! My hope for you is that you make leadership a permanent subject of study, and that you continue to learn from successful leaders in every field: business, government, science, sports, entertainment, industry, international relations, and of course, human psychology.

If you want to be a successful leader, one of the greatest things that could happen to you is that you fall in love with this exciting subject and become a lifelong student of it – because there is *always* more to learn.

Obstacles #5 and #6: Narrowmindedness and the "mirror syndrome"

These two obstacles on the road to success are like a matched pair of bookends. Narrowmindedness means overvaluing certain people because they think like you do, or because they come from similar backgrounds. The "mirror syndrome" turns that problem on its head, by assuming that everyone is automatically "like me" in how they think, approach problems, communicate, perceive things, etc. – or if they're not, they can quickly be molded into your mirror image.

These blind spots are one of the reasons why so many companies and government agencies have diversity training these days. But it's important to remember that true diversity embraces far more than just gender politics and racial and ethnic origins and identities. There is such a thing as diversity of thought, of values, of personality style and communications style. These differences are strengths, not weaknesses, for an organization.

It's good to recognize when others don't think, act or perceive in the same style that we do. But the next step is not, "How can I make them conform to my pattern?" For a successful leader, the next step is: "How can I learn from them? How should I communicate with them in ways they will value and appreciate? How can I make the best use of their unique qualities to expand our team's reach and capabilities?"

A great leader does more than pay lip service to diversity. A great leader *leverages* diversity as a valued asset.

Obstacles #7-9: Overrating harmony, popularity and consensus

These three roadblocks to your success as a leader are all related. Each of them is about getting ends and means mixed up -- putting too much stress on the means, and losing sight of the ends.

The end of leadership, its ultimate goal and value, is about making the best decisions, choosing the right goals, and inspiring and supporting your team to go out and achieve those goals.

But if you have a strong dislike of vigorous discussion, debate and even disagreement – and if you allow your feelings to prevent your team from fully thinking through the pros and cons of all the alternatives -- then you can't make the best decisions.

In a related issue, if your number-one priority is to make sure everyone likes you, you'll end up making decisions based on what other people think, not based on what's best for the organization. As a result, you'll end up telling your team members what they *want* to hear, instead of what they *need* to hear.

Finally, you might be perfectly willing to tolerate vigorous debate, and you might even be willing to live with the fact that not all team members will love you. Yet you can still insist that at the end of the day, everyone must agree on a policy or goal, before the team can move forward. This demand for 100% consensus can be paralyzing.

Even more dangerous, insisting on 100% consensus shifts responsibility for decision-making from the leader to the "lowest common denominator" of whatever idea gets buy-in from every member of the team.

This is not a formula for success; it's abdication of leadership, masquerading as "democracy."

A successful leader must have the strength to make tough decisions, without having 100% support – and sometimes without any support

– from the team, if the leader knows the decision they've made is truly the right thing to do.

One of the most powerful and effective leaders of the 20th century was British Prime Minister Margaret Thatcher, known as "the Iron Lady" for her tough, no-nonsense leadership style. Lady Thatcher was no fan of consensus. She famously said:

"Consensus is the process of abandoning all beliefs, principles, values, and policies in search of something in which no one believes, but to which no one objects; the process of avoiding the very issues that have to be solved, merely because you cannot get agreement on the way ahead. What great cause would have been fought and won under the banner: 'I stand for consensus?'"

Obstacle #10: Lack of authenticity

The final roadblock that I have repeatedly seen on the road to successful leadership is, to be blunt, hypocrisy. There are some leaders (or would-be leaders) who put on a false front, pretending to be one kind of person or to live one kind of life, while actually being and living something very different.

(This is particularly easy and popular in the age of social media. Thanks to Facebook, Twitter, Instagram and the rest, putting on a false front has become a sport and an artform practiced by tens of millions of people).

For a while, a would-be leader may get away with creating a false persona for others to admire. But when you work with someone on a regular basis, it is inevitable that sooner or later, the truth comes out -- and then the "great pretender" loses the respect of their team, their clients and allies, and the company as a whole.

I once knew a guy we'll call "Max." He presented himself as a person who had everything together: a great family life, sound personal finances, and a healthy, admirable lifestyle. But slowly people began to notice odd things about Max that did not add up.

After a couple of years, it became clear that Max actually had a lot of problems including marital difficulties, significant personal debt, and – according to reliable reports -- some unhealthy habits involving substance abuse. A completely different picture of Max emerged than the one he'd been presenting all along.

The impact of these revelations on Max's career was devastating. The trust that others had put in him was shattered, not only among his team and other company leaders, but also among management and across large segments of the industry. In less than a year, Max plummeted from near the top of the company's sales rankings, to near the bottom.

Don't get me wrong: anyone can have financial or marriage problems; and a person's lifestyle, so long as it's legal, is their own choice. But creating a false persona, whether in person or online, is effectively making a declaration to others that says, "I don't respect you enough to tell you the truth, and I don't think you're smart enough to figure out that I'm lying to you."

We all know that in personal relationships, trust is the coin of the realm. But the best business relationships are also personal relationships! That's true regardless of whether it's with team members or higher-ups, customers or suppliers. (And it's equally true in government, the arts, science and all other fields).

This means that we must live with the same integrity in our business or public lives, that we live with when it comes to our personal lives. Successful leadership, like a successful personal life, is built on trust, which is built on truth and respect.

How can you see past your own blind spots? Rely on someone else's eyes!

You might ask, "How is a person supposed to notice their own blind spots? When I read about the 10 roadblocks, I have a vague inkling that I might have an issue with one or two. But how can I know for sure? How can I get complete insight into my problem? And, what can I do about it?"

This is where having a mentor proves invaluable. A good mentor is one who knows you and understands what makes you tick, appreciates your strengths and weaknesses, and is rooting for you to achieve your goals. Ideally, they also have wider experience than you, a body of knowledge they can call on to give you advice when you need it.

A great mentor has all of that, plus your permission to tell you things about yourself that may be difficult to hear.

I have made it point to have at least one formal coaching relationship through my whole career. In most cases, I pay somebody to be my coach. My coaches have changed over the years as my situation has evolved. With my current coach, we get on the phone once a month and discuss the issues I'm having or situations I'm facing.

My coach asks questions that I might not have thought of, or provides a perspective I could not have come up with on my own. In this way, he helps me become a better leader.

In addition, I have a number of informal mentors, including friends. Whenever I need help, I'll pick up the phone and say, "Hey, Larry, what would you do in this situation?"

Even if you can't afford to pay a professional coach, you can usually find someone who will listen to your problems now and then for no charge. Just make sure you pick a successful, qualified person before you start implementing their advice!

In addition, you can make use of role models from the media or from history. Choose someone you admire. Study their lives, careers and leadership styles. When you run into a challenge, ask yourself: "What would my role model do in this situation?"

Next step: begin your journey by choosing your destination

Once you have cleared the path of these 10 roadblocks, it's time to begin your journey to leadership in earnest. The next step on your path to becoming Tomorrow's Leader is to choose your destination – which is about having the _vision_ to see what your future could be, or should be.

CHAPTER 5

Every great path leads to a great destination

A successful leader has a <u>vision</u> – a clear, compelling picture of where the organization should go and how to get there.

One of the most powerful and successful leaders on the planet is someone you may never have heard of, unless you are a regular reader of financial news.

From 2014 to 2019, publications such as *Forbes*, *Fortune*, *Time* and several others consistently ranked Indian-American business leader Indra Nooyi as "the world's second most powerful woman in business" – or simply as "one of the most powerful women on earth," period.

Indra Nooyi was chairman and CEO of PepsiCo for 12 years. During her tenure, she increased the company's sales by 80%. How did she achieve this stunning performance? Well, the truth is that Indra did nearly everything right. But three of her most important moves were:

1) When she first became CEO, she recognized and frankly acknowledged that PepsiCo faced serious challenges.

2) She came up with a big, bold, exciting – but achievable – vision for a new and very different future for the company.

3) She inspired her management team (and persuaded her investors) to support her with 100% commitment to do whatever was required to make her vision into a reality.

There are many leadership lessons in Indra's career, but one of the most important is the crucial importance of <u>vision</u>. Great leaders know that having or not having a vision makes the difference between purposeful activity and drifting...between real progress, versus just running around putting out fires.

So in this chapter, we'll explore the role of <u>vision</u>: what it is, what it's not, why it's important, how to develop it, and how to know if you have successfully created a shared vision among your team.

To get clear on these concepts, we'll take a closer look at Indra Nooyi's story in her own words.

Vision often begins, as it did for Indra Nooyi, by recognizing there's a problem...or an opportunity

"When I looked at the world when I became CEO," says Indra, "I saw some trends which worried me."[6]

For a multinational company based on snack foods and soft drinks, one of the most worrisome trends was growing consumer concerns over health and wellness. This was leading to an emphasis on prevention and healthier eating. Consumers were buying less salty, high-fat foods and sugary drinks. If this trend continued, where would it leave PepsiCo?

Other troubling trends on Indra's radar as she took the reins of the company were greater stress on environmental issues such as water rights, greenhouse gasses and landfills. Regulatory requirements around the world were ratcheting up, and consumer movements in favor of "clean and green" manufacturing were becoming very popular.

---

6   "Indra Nooyi On Being One of the Longest -Serving Female CEOs," interview with *Fortune* magazine's Nina Easton, Sept. 16, 2019; https://www.youtube.com/watch?v=vRy-_w4cvT8&list=PLXD2YeVTziWW92UZiDW-IQH17h4X-7DNx&index=23

Finally, Indra saw clearly that PepsiCo needed to develop a more inclusive, welcoming workforce to reflect an increasingly diverse global market and to enable the company to retain more its best people.

Indra knew that failing to address any one of these issues could seriously hurt PepsiCo. The company had to respond fast and smart. As she put it: "I knew we had to take a great company and make it greater."

This is where vision begins for many successful leaders. They see a problem that they want to solve, or desperately need to solve. Alternatively, they may see an opportunity to improve on an existing product or service, or they may imagine a brand-new product or service that no one has ever seen before, but which they'll love as soon as they are introduced to it. (Apple iPhone, anyone?)

Whether the vision is sparked by problems or opportunities, the leader ends up asking herself the same basic questions: "How can things be better? What would the world look like, if this problem were solved? What need is going unmet, or could be satisfied in a better way?"

Asking these questions are the birth pangs of a powerful vision.

On the journey of leadership, vision represents the ultimate destination

As Indra considered the situation for PepsiCo in 2006, she saw that solving PepsiCo's problems was going to require the company to make some big changes. She envisioned a new, improved company that was more health-friendly, more environmentally friendly, and more employee-friendly.

Indra called her vision, "Performance with a Purpose," meaning – *We're not just going to make money. Yes, we'll earn great profits, both in the short term and in the long term. But we'll also do what's right for our customers' health, what's right for the health of the planet, and what's right for the long-term health of the company.*

This was Indra's vision for where she wanted the company to go. These are simple ideas, but they are powerful. In fact, their simplicity is part of why they have so much power. Anyone can instantly see the value in going to this destination. Anyone can get excited about living in this new world and working for this stronger company that makes better products.

Notice that Indra's vision was a <u>destination</u>, not a road map. She did not spell out specific goals such as, "We're going to reduce the salt in Lay's Potato Chips by 18% over the next three years" or "We'll eliminate aspartame from Diet Pepsi."

She left those specifics to the next stage. This is true of every great vision promoted by a leader. So when you're working out the vision that will drive your leadership, ask yourself: "Where should we go? Why? What will it look like when we get there? How will it feel?"

When you have a clear, compelling answer to those questions, you have a clear, compelling vision for your team or your organization. Once you have a great destination in mind, then it's time to create the road map for how to get there.

Your mission statement translates your vision into actionable steps

How did Indra plan to lead PepsiCo to this future destination of a healthier company serving healthier consumers on a healthier planet? She outlined a simple road map for her team:

"We set about doing things like reducing the fat, sugar and salt in our products, without sacrificing taste," she said. "[We said], we'll still deliver [a strong financial] performance...[but at the same time,] we're going to reduce our plastics use and reduce our greenhouse gasses. [And to increase our diversity and retention rates], we're going to make this a great company for everybody who wants to work here, not just a few people."

This amounts to a mission statement, which serves the vision. But the mission statement is where the rubber meets the road. The questions you ask yourself are different at this stage: "How will we reach our destination? How will we make this great future a reality? What will be our strategy and tactics?"

Maybe you don't know how to get there yet. You may not have a clear sense of how your vision will make money. That's okay. You can come up with that later, or discover it by trial and error. These are questions that you can and should share with your team.

Remember, when Sergey Brin and Larry Page launched Google, they did not know how it would generate revenues. It took them a couple of years to figure out that monetization of their product was about highly targeted advertising.

Far more important than knowing precisely how your idea will make money, is knowing precisely what problem you're trying to solve. Many would-be leaders, especially in business but also in other fields, have "crashed" because they fell in love with a solution or a technology or a market. Then they designed a product or even launched an organization, long before they really understood whether or not their idea filled a real need in the market, or solved an important problem in the world that was worth solving. A cool idea, by itself, is not a vision!

A powerful vision attracts followers all by itself. It can even provide the ammunition you need to convince skeptics

When you share your vision with others, not everyone may rush to embrace it. Some may feel it's too expensive. Others may claim it will take too long, or require too much focus, or it's just unnecessary.

Even the greatest leaders have experienced this kind of internal opposition. Often the more brilliant and revolutionary the vision, the stiffer the pushback.

Back in the late 1920s, Henry Ford gathered his top engineers and announced that he wanted them to create the world's first economical, mass-production V8 engine for a consumer automobile that middle-class drivers could afford. His engineers said it was impossible.

Ford stuck to his vision. He made his team keep coming up with new ideas. His passionate belief in the idea, and his arguments for the improved power and efficiency of the new engine, inspired his engineers to keep trying new approaches. Eventually they succeeded.[7]

Like Henry Ford, Indra Nooyi also ran into a certain amount of initial opposition when she outlined her vision and her road map to PepsiCo's board of directors and its major investors. Nevertheless, she knew she was on the right track because her management team was excited by the possibilities. She explains:

"People on our team actually embraced [the vision] and said, 'We have to do this.' Because they were hearing it from their family members, who said things have to change...[These team members knew that by signing up for my vision], they were creating a long-term, sustainably performing company."

But the board and the investors were another story, said Indra. They were more interested in the short-term profit performance. "All of [the changes I wanted to make] required investment," she said. "R&D investments [in new food and beverage formulas], investments to figure out to reduce the water use. So I told [my major stockholders and fund managers], this is what we're going to invest....They said, 'You're not Mother Teresa! Why do you have to reduce the fat, sugar and salt?'"

Indra used the power of the vision itself to win over the skeptics. She recalls, "I looked at them and said, 'Have you changed your eating or drinking habits?'" The skeptics admitted that they had changed their own consumption patterns, and that was how she persuaded them that PepsiCo had no choice but to get ahead of this curve.

---

7   "The Ford V8: Henry Ford's Final Triumph." Bill McGuire, *Autoweek*, June 5, 2003. https://www.autoweek.com/news/a2098616/ford-v8-henry-fords-final-triumph/

To be motivating, the vision must be advanced by a leader whom the team or organization believes in

Having a great vision is a crucial requirement for successful leadership, but by itself, it's not enough. The leader herself must command sufficient respect to give people confidence that the vision can and will be realized.

Otherwise, would-be followers may ask themselves: "Why should I commit to this vision? How do I know my leader will provide me the tools and resources I need to get the job done? How do I know they won't pull the rug out from me and change the vision two weeks from now? Also, what's in it for me? Why should I make the effort to support this goal?"

Performance and personal integrity are the only persuasive answers to some of these questions. But other questions should be answered as part of the vision itself. Such as: "To make sure we have the resources we need to pursue and achieve this vision, I am committing the following investments to this goal."

And: "If we all commit to realizing this vision, by the end of next year we'll have achieved XYZ in our revenue structure, and you'll see a commensurate reward for your contribution reflected in your bonus."

To communicate your vision, tell a simple story that everyone on your team can repeat. Then repeat it yourself!

A successful leader must be able to articulate their vision just as Indra Nooyi did – in clear, simple terms that anyone can understand and repeat.

An important test of whether your team understands the vision is to ask individual members to explain it to you. If they all express it clearly and correctly, then you have communicated your vision effectively and there is an excellent chance that everyone in the boat will be rowing in the same direction.

But if every person has a wildly different take on the vision, or it's vague and incomplete, then you have a problem. In most cases, this is probably not the fault of the followers; it's more likely to be a signal that the leader needs to work on telling the story in simpler, clearer terms.

A great vision does not require complex, convoluted words and ideas. "Make great-tasting products that have less fat, salt and sugar" is easy to grasp and repeat. "Design a V8 engine that millions of American auto owners can afford," is as simple as it gets.

You might be surprised to learn just how much time and effort successful business leaders put into creating the "story" that conveys their vision. But if you are leading people to a totally new and different destination, then a story is all you have – and it had better be good!

Steve Jobs was famous for his Apple product launch presentations, which were elaborately scripted "one-man theater." Other CEOs may have fulltime storytellers on the payroll who work with them through 50 or 100 drafts of a story before they're confident that they can tell it well, and that listeners will instantly understand the vision and get excited.

Once the "vision story" is nailed down, telling it once is only the beginning. The story must be told and retold, with variations and reminders, and preferably with memorable language.

For example, Indra Nooyi summed up her story in that catchphrase which she worked into countless speeches, memos, and internal company documents: "Performance with a Purpose." She explained the philosophy behind the catchphrase again and again. She updated her story with fresh examples every time PepsiCo succeeded with a new, healthier beverage or an innovative, eco-friendly packaging advance.

When a vision is translated into a vivid story and a memorable catchphrase, it takes on a life of its own. It enters the company's bloodstream; it informs your team's thinking and guides their decisions. It plays a key role in defining the company's culture.

How many times is enough to repeat the vision? As professional communicators often say, "About the time you're getting sick of hearing the message, in most cases that's when your audience is just beginning to really pay attention and wake up to realize the real meaning and importance of what you're saying."

You should repeat the story of the vision until you start seeing and hearing evidence that your team or organization has incorporated it into their thinking, and they are explaining their own actions and decisions in terms of the vision.

The practical, pragmatic impact of sharing a clear and powerful vision

Surprisingly, perhaps, not every leader is convinced of the value of having a vision and the importance of being able to inspire your team to commit to it. For example, President George H.W. Bush famously dismissed the whole subject as "the vision thing." He thought leadership was about making the right decisions and executing them well, period. The whole idea of "vision" in his opinion was about campaigning, sales and marketing, sloganeering, a form of advertising – nothing he liked or respected or cared about.

Bush was half right; making good decisions and executing them well is a huge part of successful leadership. But Bush lost his bid for a second term in the White House to a naturally gifted communicator named Bill Clinton who worked extremely hard at communicating his vision of America to the voters.

A clear, powerful vision can get you a job. It can fire up your team and attract their best efforts. It can overcome skeptics and critics. It can attract substantial investment (don't believe me? Watch any episode of "Shark Tank.")

Most importantly, a powerful vision can provide the energy and inspiration to transform your team, your organization, or the whole world.

A template for vision, mission, strategy and tactics: the Civil Rights Movement of the 1960s

One of the most successful visions ever offered in human history was articulated in its most powerful form on August 28th, 1963 on the steps of the Lincoln Memorial in Washington, DC. That's when Dr. Martin Luther King, Jr. gave his famous "I Have a Dream" speech to a rally of civil rights supporters and activists.

King's oratory laid out the vision of a color-blind world in terms that still thrill and inspire listeners today. King spoke of a world where justice prevailed, where equal rights and equal opportunity were guaranteed to all people, and where individuals are judged "not by the color of their skin, but by the content of their character."

This famous speech also helps us understand the difference between the *vision* and the *mission* -- and how both of them translate into *strategy* and *tactics.*

In this case, the vision was a color-blind world; the mission was to change the laws and culture of the United States to ensure equal rights become built into our society and its institutions.

The vision is where you want to go. The mission is the roadmap for how you get there. It's the concrete, specific goals and objectives you pursue to move, step by step, toward achieving the vision.

Next comes strategy. In Gandhi's words, Dr. King knew he had to "make the injustice visible" in order to stir the conscience of the nation. Finally comes tactics -- in this case, nonviolent civil resistance and peaceful protests that provoked a brutal response from police in full sight of TV news cameras. Civil rights leaders and movement members knew this would result in the broadcasting of highly disturbing images into every American living room...creating political support for the laws desired by the movement...which then created the legal conditions to begin realizing the just world of the vision.

Vision, mission, strategy and tactics: these are the structure of every successful journey to becoming Tomorrow's Leader!

CHAPTER 6

When you come to a fork in the road, make a decision!

The job of a leader is to make decisions. If you want to make great decisions, you need a great decision-making process.

A couple of guys named Reed Hastings and Marc Randolph are the mega-successful founders and leaders of one of the world's largest, most successful entertainment companies.

Never heard of Hastings and Randolph? Well, you have certainly heard of their organization. It's called Netflix, and as of the year 2020 it is a $20 billion global empire.

These two business leaders founded Netflix in 1997. They launched it on a fast growth trajectory by the simple expedient of giving customers what they want. But the two founders knew what they wanted, too: "We wanted to be the amazon.com of something," admitted Randolph.[8]

Hastings put it a little differently: "When you grow up, as I have, in the shadow of Steve Jobs, Bill Gates and others, success is defined as the total global transformation of a market. To achieve that, you need low prices and an attractive offering. It's about trying to make a positive impact on a big scale."

---

8   https://www.washingtonpost.com/opinions/five-myths-about-netflix/2014/02/21/787c7c8e-9a3f-11e3-b931-0204122c514b_story.html?utm_term=.b4f117558d14

After looking around at various possibilities for sell-by-mail merchandise, the two leaders settled on DVDs, which were just hitting the market that year. (By the way, Hastings and Randolph also have a great "origin myth" about how they got the idea for Netflix. It's an oft-told story that one of them now admits is just that, a myth. We'll get to that later on.)

The power of great decisions

Hastings and Randolph built their phenomenal company, and kept it growing at astonishing rates, by being excellent decision-makers. Netflix itself is one of the great "disruptive innovations" in today's business world, and its repeated explosions of growth can be traced through a series of five brilliant decisions – three of which are well-known, and two of which are rarely talked about.

Making great decisions is the key responsibility of a great leader. It is the ultimate test of leadership.

If you want to know how to make truly great decisions in your own life, I strongly advise you to take a page from Reed Hastings and Marc Randolph. Regardless of whether you happen to run a billion-dollar corporation, a small team, the local PTA, a family, or if you simply want to exercise the best possible self-leadership -- allow me to share Hasting's and Randolph's amazing story.

Disruptive decision #1: Take on giant, established companies, using a new business model

When Hastings and Randolph launched Netflix, they had plenty of entrenched competition. The most obvious was Blockbuster, which dominated video rentals in the 1980s and '90s. Around the time Netflix began, Blockbuster was a $3 billion giant with 25,000+ employees, not to mention a chain of 8,000 stores and 6,000 rental kiosks.

Hastings and Randolph decided <u>not</u> to try to duplicate Blockbuster's brick and mortar distribution chain, but to do every transaction by mail, like Amazon and to a lesser extent, Walmart.

After two years of trying to "out-Amazon Amazon" and failing, the Netflix guys decided to challenge the status quo with a new and different strategy: drop sales and focus on rentals. Also, drop per-day charges and have a set subscription fee, with no due dates and no late fees. Netflix was still a ship-by-mail business at that point, but at last they were on the way to a giant success by offering something consumers loved.

(About that "origin myth"...Reed Hastings has often told the story that he got the idea for Netflix because he was a loyal Blockbuster customer who got sick and tired of paying late fees for returning movies a couple of days late. Supposedly Hastings racked up $40 in fines on just one rental, "Apollo 13," and he decided "enough is enough!"

But Marc Randolph, who left the company in 2003, admits this story was concocted to give the new company a feisty, upstart image – and a grievance that consumers could identify with.[9] In fact, Netflix began with late fees, too.[10]

This kind of corporate mythmaking is nothing new. The famous story about eBay originally being founded as a way to sell Pez candy dispensers is another such myth.)

Disruptive decision #2: Shift focus from rent-by-mail to streaming technology, backed by a powerhouse algorithm

In theory, any competitor with enough funds should be able to set up a lookalike company and steal Netflix's business (Amazon is

---

9   https://www.cnbc.com/2017/05/23/netflix-ceo-reed-hastings-on-how-the-company-was-born.html

10   Op cit., Washington Post.

certainly trying). But Netflix has several advantages that are difficult to overcome.

First, they aggressively adopted a "blue ocean," "get there firstest with the mostest" strategy. As broadband Internet service became more widely available in the early 2000s, Netflix took note as YouTube demonstrated the viability (and incredible popularity) of streaming content -- even if they were only cat videos.

Seeing this, Netflix was quick out of the box in 2007 with something then unheard-of: full video streaming services for Hollywood movies. They offered streaming as an instant-gratification alternative to rent-by-mail, where DVDs took a day or two to arrive, and often longer.

In addition, Netflix created an unbeatable "suggestion algorithm" or recommendation engine that gets to know each customer's individual tastes and preferences. Customers love it. Fully 75% of subscriber rentals come from this algorithm's highly personalized recommendations.

Disruptive decision #3: Get into original programming and become a content producer on a large scale

The Netflix leaders gradually realized that they would continue to be as colorless as Hertz and Avis, and would have equally weak customer loyalty, until they started doing the equivalent of building their own cars – or in this case, producing their own entertainment content.

The company flirted with original content production starting in 2004, but shut it down after a few years. They admitted that they had to make a bigger, stronger commitment to programming if they were going to have a transformative impact on their image, one that could build more brand awareness and lock in customer loyalty.

Armed with the lessons of their first (failed) attempt, they came back to original programming in 2012 on an all-out basis, funding "House of Cards" as an original Netflix series for a whopping $100 million.

Today Reed Hastings freely admits this move was not a guaranteed win. Company leaders knew they were taking a huge risk: "We weren't confident...we were like, holy (shit)! That was scary."[11]

Disruptive decision #4: Don't sell advertising

This is a biggie. Netflix's decision to forgo the potential to rake in billions of additional dollars from advertising every year is an "invisible strategy," in the sense that few consumers ever think about it.

It would be easy for Netflix to stream an advertisement that plays before every movie begins on a consumer's monitor or mobile. They could even have ads that pop up in the middle of the movie, just like commercial TV networks have ad breaks in the middle of each program.

But consumers would hate it. And, it would complicate what is now a beautifully simple business, forcing Netflix to customize streaming movies with different ads (and different prices charged to advertisers) in different countries and different markets.

"These things which seem like low-hanging fruit never are," Marc Randolph commented. "Ads are a distraction, never an additive thing."[12]

Still, the temptation must have been great to put aside all those objections and take the money. Ever since Google proved the power of advertising to support digital content by leveraging precisely targeted audience segments, probably 50% of all the digital startups in the world have answered the question, "How are you going to make money?" by pointing to Google and saying, "We're going to sell advertising, just like Larry and Sergey."

---

11 https://www.ted.com/talks/reed_hastings_how_netflix_changed_entertainment_and_where_it_s_headed/up-next
12 https://bgr.com/2019/09/17/netflix-vs-blockbuster-marc-randolph-interview-reed-hastings/

Disruptive decision #5: Take on $20 billion in debt

Netflix may generate $20 billion a year in revenues, but its long-term debt adds up to just about the same amount. Are they worried? Not particularly. Their stellar growth rate seems to be racing ahead of their debt service payments just fine, thank you very much.

And, Netflix is hardly the only entertainment giant to roll the dice by borrowing huge sums of money. Back in 1936, as the Walt Disney Co. was making its 1937 blockbuster animated feature "Snow White," company CFO Roy Disney warned his brother Walt that they were in serious trouble. They owed their bank $1 million, an astronomical sum back then.

Instead of being worried, Walt broke into a huge grin. "Can you imagine banks loaning a million dollars to a couple of yokels like us?" he asked Roy. "Boy, we have really arrived!"

Today of course The Walt Disney Company generates about $70 billion in annual revenues with total equity of $93 billion.

Decisions are usually far more complex than they look

What can we learn from the story of Netflix? A great deal.

Perhaps the most important takeaway is that a decision is rarely a simple yes/no, stay-or-go, up-or-down set of alternatives – even if it looks that way at first glance. In reality, decisions are a complex, sophisticated exercise in learning, thinking and acting – all bundled into one. Making good decisions requires a deep knowledge of the situation, and a subtle understanding of the range of possibilities and likely consequences.

In other words, decision-making is chess, where a dozen factors or more all influence each other at once. It's not a coin toss, where it's either heads or tails. Put another way, decision-making is poker, where the consistent winners are the ones who count the cards, evaluate the odds, and learn to read the other players. It's not black-jack, where your only choices are to either say "Hit me" or stand pat, and where outcomes are purely mechanistic.

For all these reasons, the most effective business leaders – and the most effective leaders in any field, from war to art, science and edu-cation -- have a standard list of criteria they use to make smart, effective decisions.

10 guidelines for successful decision-making

1) *Know the market or the terrain. Especially be alert to large-scale evolution in the environment, from new technology to new consumer tastes to new regulatory requirements, new sources of competition, etc.*

   • Hastings and Randolph understood that broadband and streaming video were not only changing the technology base; they were also changing customer expectations. Their move to streaming movies leveraged this knowledge.

2) *Clearly understand the problem you're trying to solve. Failure to get this step right frequently dooms the entire effort.*

   • Hastings and Randolph gave themselves a very simple problem to solve: how can we delight customers by providing entertainment in the simplest, fastest, most convenient, customer-friendly way?

3) *Once you have a clear understanding of the problem, explore the alternatives for solutions to that problem.*

   • Ideally you explore alternative solutions "on paper," but often there is no substitute for trying something in the real world -- especially in markets like entertainment, food and beverage, etc. where customer reactions are totally unpredictable, even if you do extensive polling. Just ask Fox studios about "Star Wars," which pre-release polls said would be a flop. Also ask the Cola-Cola Company about "New Coke," which taste tests predicted would be a sure-fire hit.

If you have to actually launch a venture in the real world to find out if it works, try a small pilot program if possible. But as Hastings and Randolph learned with their first foray into content, there are cases where you have to "go big or go home." (See point 9 below regarding commitment.)

4) *Find out when, where -- and above all, WHY -- similar solutions have worked before. Or, if they failed, find out why they failed, and why this time it's going to be different.*

- Hastings and Randolph knew what didn't work: Blockbuster. They knew what did work: Amazon. What they had to figure out was how to be like Amazon, only better, in one particular niche.

5) *Study the timing. Understand when the timing is right. Why is NOW the best time to make this decision? If you put off making the decision, will you get more clarity? Or will you just lose opportunities and surrender some of your freedom for action?*

- Hastings and Randolph jumped into the movie rental business just before DVDs began to arrive on the market. But 10 years before they had seen CDs rapidly replace audio cassettes, and they knew all the same factors were lined up to make DVDs a success. They founded Netflix even before they got their hands on a DVD because they knew the first-mover advantage was critical to success. Truly, timing is everything.

In same vein, however, they held off on "going big" with homegrown content for several years, until they felt they had a strong grasp of how to succeed in that arena.

6) *Consult your team. Get their perspective. Really listen. There are many ways to do this, from a decentralized decision-making structure with shared responsibility, to a structure where the leader consults the team, then makes key decisions on their own. In the latter case, the team will be far more willing to support you, if they know their views have been heard and respected – even if you ultimately decide to go another direction.*

- Netflix has chosen to go the decentralized, shared-power route. Reed Hastings says teamwork and information-sharing are basic pillars of the company's leadership structure.

"[When we established Netflix] I was super-focused on how to run [the company] with no process, but not have chaos. So we developed all these mechanisms: super high-talented people, alignment, talking openly, sharing information. Internally, people are stunned at how much information [we share with everyone, including] all the core strategies... Our culture is big on shared responsibility."[13]

7) *Once you come up with a specific action plan to implement your decision, evaluate the risks of launching the plan. Then, evaluate the risks of <u>not</u> launching it. This includes a cost-benefit analysis. Is the game worth the candle?*

- Netflix knew that becoming a large-scale content producer would be hugely expensive and financially risky. The landscape is littered with failed movie studios and TV production houses, often led by very talented professionals.

But Netflix decided that the upside of this risk was so important, and that their relationship to their customers was so deep and powerful, that they had no choice but to take the gamble if they wanted to continue growing to

---

13   <u>TED.com, op cit.</u>

become a dominant force in the world of entertainment, not just a conveyer belt for someone else's product.

8) *When conditions seem right, commit to the plan and launch it. This is the key decision-making step. "Commit" doesn't mean sticking your big toe in the water. It means diving in and starting to swim for the far shore.*

If the objective is important enough, and if potential rewards are big enough, and if your cost-benefit analysis comes up positive, then spend the money. Hire the people. Restructure the organization if necessary. Take the risk. Commit! If you don't commit, you haven't really made a decision — you're just playing at making a decision.

- Again, Netflix made a $100 million commitment to its groundbreaking TV series, "House of Cards." The company has since greatly expanded its entertainment content portfolio.

  Like Disney, Netflix realized that "content is king" and that media can have an enormous social impact on leisure time, customer enjoyment, cultural norms, and even more socially conscious goals like improving childhood education.

9) *Stay alert to fast-changing, up-to-the-minute, localized conditions. In other words: Don't launch your Titanic in an ice storm. Or, if icebergs show up halfway into the voyage, be prepared to slow down and change course.*

- When Netflix was founded, streaming video was barely on the horizon and was considered far in the future. When it did begin to appear, the leading movie and TV studios screamed that they would never, never, never permit their content to be released in this channel.

  Ignoring all that, Netflix recognized the reality that consumers were moving into the digital world, and content providers would have no choice but to follow them. The changeover had already happened with music when Netflix switched to streaming in 1997. The company nimbly jumped onto this new platform and quickly established itself as the king of streaming Hollywood video entertainment.

10) *Constantly reevaluate. Stay in "perpetual learning mode." Be mentally and materially ready to adjust your short-term goals and tactics on the fly, in the moment, as circumstances develop and as you learn from experience.*

As General Dwight Eisenhower said, "No battle plan survives contact with the enemy. Before the battle, plans are everything. Once the battle begins, plans are worthless."

- When Netflix first started, Hastings and Randolph did not pretend to have all the answers. But they certainly knew the right questions: What would be their business model? What technology would they rely on? Exactly what would their customer relationships look like? All of these factors, and much more, were discovered and repeatedly redefined as continual "works in progress."

What about leaders who believe in making decisions by "gut instinct"?

The rules of successful decision-making outlined here may sound like a lot of work. That's because they are! But they're worth it. And, they are the soundest basis I know for a decision with the best chance of being truly successful.

How can we be sure that's true? Because if you study the careers of great leaders and decision-makers from Steve Jobs to Napoleon, and from Estée Lauder to Elon Musk, you will see these 10 patterns emerging again and again.

Of course, there are some highly successful leaders who claim they never bother with such detailed, analytical, right-brain approaches to making a big decision. A famous example is Sony's longtime chairman Akio Morita, who famously claimed to make all big decisions based on pure gut instinct.

"At night before I go to bed, I swallow the deal," he said. "In the morning when I wake up, if I feel good, I know it's a good deal and we go forward with it. But if I wake up with a stomachache, then I know something is wrong with the deal and either we fix it or we walk away from it."[14]

No doubt Morita was telling the absolute truth when he made this claim. But by the time he became Chairman of Sony Corporation, he possessed a highly educated gut! Whenever a deal was put before him, he had probably seen literally 1,000 other opportunities just like it before, and thought through them all. This means Morita-san did not just swallow the deal; before that he had also "swallowed" the decision-making criteria. Thanks to internalizing these processes, he could do "by instinct" what most of us need to consciously think about.

This brings us right back to the Competency Ladder, which we discussed in Chapter 4. Akio Morita had reached the point of being "unconsciously competent" as a decision-maker. All of us can aspire to get there someday. When we're just starting out, however, we'll probably need to practice climbing the lower steps of the ladder a few times!

That said, gut instinct is important. I've met many leaders who said, "I made a few decisions that turned out to be mistakes. In each instance, I knew going in that something didn't feel quite right, but I ignored those feelings and pressed forward anyway – and it cost me."

My advice for leaders is: Don't automatically go with your gut, but also never ignore your gut. If something feels wrong to you, it

---

14   Paraphrase from Akio Morita's autobiography, "Made in Japan."

probably is – even if you can't put your finger on it. Listen to your instincts and respect your intuition, along with all the analytical, conscious decision-making tools at your disposal.

Some final quick pointers for successful decision-making

Even if you fully embrace the 10 guidelines suggested here, there are still many decision-making traps that the most conscientious leader can fall into. At the same time, there are a handful of surprisingly simple decision-making tips that can contribute to greater success.

Here are a few of each.

Procrastination: You can always justify a delay in decision-making for "more study" or "waiting for better conditions." Leaders who drag their feet and refuse to make a decision eventually impose a terrible burden on their team. The leader's fear of making a mistake can bring a company to a halt, where nobody is able to move forward in any direction because they don't know what the decision will be. Beware of "paralysis by analysis."

Echo chamber: Consulting your team about a major decision is a good, all things being equal, but it requires having a team of people that includes some with different backgrounds and perspectives than your own. There is no value in a roomful of "yes men" and "yes women." As the saying goes, "If two minds think exactly alike, one of them is unnecessary." Don't just seek out different voices; seek out different points of view.

Communicate: Once a major decision is made, the leader's job is to clearly communicate that decision, why it was made, and what each person's role will be in carrying out the decision. It's important to connect the dots and explain what factors went into making the decision, especially if it's a controversial choice or a tough new path. This kind of frankness is crucial both for effective teamwork and for morale.

Short-term thinking: It can be a serious problem to make decisions that have long-term impact, based solely on short-term effects. An obvious example is when a person jumps from one job to another, simply because it pays better – and regardless of all other considerations. But if you hate the work, or don't respect the company, or if you commit yourself to a grueling commute, or you give up the opportunity for future career development, this kind of decision-making can be extremely costly and even self-defeating.

360-degree view: Before making a decision, look at it from many different perspectives. If you're a leader in an organization, ask yourself: If we make this decision, how will the other leaders feel? How will this impact them? What will this do for our employees? What will it do for the staff? How will it be perceived? Who will like it, who will not? Why? How will this decision look to our clients? How will it look to the public? A decision that is considered from all angles, is nearly always a better decision.

The 'USA Today' test: One of the angles you should consider, should be: How will this decision look if it's reported on the front page of tomorrow's *USA Today,* or becomes the lead story on *ABC World News Tonight?* Is this something we will be proud of, that our employees will be excited about, and that our shareholders will support? Things can look just fine when you're considering them in the privacy of your own mind or within the sanctuary of the office environment, but then look very different if blared in full view of a hyper-critical media or a volatile, excitable public.

The Domino Effect and the Ripple Effect: A couple of related ways to reframe a pending decision is to consider these two ways of measuring the likely effects of going forward with that action or policy.

The Domino Effect traces the probable consequences sequentially in time: "If we do A, then the likely result will be B, which will cause C, which will trigger D, and then lead to E." If you don't feel good about E, then you might want to rethink A!

The Ripple Effect is first cousin to the 360-degree view. It's about making sure you consider the immediate impact (not over time) that a decision may have on other people, departments, organizations and realms of society. But while the 360-degree view was mostly about predicting feelings and perceptions, the Ripple Effect is about being cognizant of more pragmatic, measurable organizational reverberations.

For example: "If we do A, then we'll have to shift around resources among departments B and C, which will have a financial impact on organization D, which may well affect the performance and outcome relating to goals E, F and G." Don't forget to include opportunity cost in this equation.

The 10-10-10 rule: One of the simplest and yet most effective yardsticks that I recommend for evaluating a decision is this rule. Ask yourself, If I make this decision, how will I feel about it in 10 minutes? How will I feel in 10 months? How am I likely to feel about it in 10 years? If you can honestly say you'll feel good at each of these "way stations," then it's probably a good decision.

The Alignment Model: When leaders evaluate a decision, they often forget the need to examine *themselves*. You don't want to make a decision that's influenced by the fact that you just had a fight with your significant other, so you're mad at the world, or depressed.

You also don't want to make a decision based on rationalizing a desire for something that works against your real goals. As in – "Yes I know I'm on a diet, but just one piece of chocolate cake can't hurt me."

To become more conscious of your own internal processes and motivations, draw a triangle and put "thoughts, emotions and actions" in the corners and "goals" in the center:

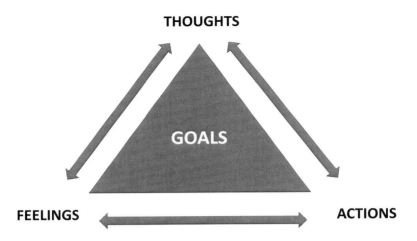

The two-way arrows prompt you to ask yourself: How are my emotions affecting my thoughts here? Conversely, how are my emotions affecting my actions? How are my actions affecting my thoughts? My emotions? How are my thoughts affecting my emotions and actions?

Above all, what impact are all of these two-directional influences having on my goals as I prepare to make this decision? Are my actions, thoughts and emotions all truly aligned with my goals right now?

If not, what is off-kilter? And how can I get everything working together so that I've got the strongest possible basis for making and implementing a decision that I'll be happy with, both in the short run and the long run?

I have found that using this Alignment Model for honest self-appraisal can be a powerful tool to help you become your best self, and commit to a course that is more likely to bring you closer to realizing your goals.

Decision-making: an art and a science

Like leadership itself, making decisions is both an art and a science. The art is about being open to new ideas and intuitions, then communicating so that others are eager to follow. The science is about getting your facts straight and your numbers nailed down, so you have the best possible basis upon which to decide.

Decision-making can be a burden or a joy. Countless leaders feel "weighed down by the awful responsibility" -- they take no pleasure in exercising leadership. On the other hand, far too many leaders use decision-making as a chance to grab power, inflate their own egos and lord it over others.

How do you find the right balance between these two extremes? Very simply, by remembering that <u>decision-making is not about you</u>.

It's about those you lead and those you serve – whether they're three members of your family, or 100 million subscribers to your Netflix service.

As the decision-maker, your job is to learn all you reasonably can, make the call that you truly believe will deliver the biggest benefits to everyone in your circle, and then work with your team to deliver those outcomes.

If you've done your homework and your heart is in the right place, people will sense it. They will support you when your decisions don't work out perfectly, and celebrate with you when your decision delivers results.

On your journey to becoming Tomorrow's Leader, decision-making is one of the most important milestones – and one of the toughest to do well. There is no getting around it, decision-making requires courage because it requires putting yourself, and your team, on the line.

One of the keenest insights into decision-making that I've ever seen, is attributed to Yama Mubtaker, a Canadian expert on sustainable international development. Yama said:

"Decision-making is power.

Most people don't have the guts to make a tough decision because they want to make the 'right decision' and so they make no decision.

"Remember, life is short, so do things that matter the most and have the courage to make tough decisions and to chase your dreams."

CHAPTER 7

You will cover a wide variety of terrain on the road to successful leadership

In today's highly diverse society and fast-changing economy, the best leaders use a variety of leadership styles, not just one.

One of the worst business leaders I ever heard of, bar none, was an enormous egotist who thought of himself as one of the *best* and *smartest* CEOs on the planet. For purposes of this story, we'll call this leader "George" – which is not his real name, obviously!

"George" ran a very small company that made a highly popular product for a specialty business, connected with the entertainment industry. The company's core staff was composed of seven super-competent, super-dedicated people. Each of these team members had remarkable talents in their particular areas of responsibility, and they took extraordinary pride in their work.

George's team turned out a product that was universally acknowledged by their industry to be clearly superior to the competition. What's more, this team improved their product every single year. In addition, this group of specialists was a model of close cooperation. They supported each other instinctively and automatically.

At this point you may be wondering -- if George was such a terrible leader, how did he attract such great people?

There are three answers. First, the company was located in one of America's largest cities, so it had access to a tremendous talent pool that was geared to its glamorous industry — a sector that countless people were eager to work in. Second, to his credit, George recognized talent when he saw it; and he paid well. Third, George allowed his team members a great deal of autonomy in their various roles.

If George had simply focused on the big strategic leadership issues, providing high-level guidance and support to his outstanding team while allowing them to continue doing their jobs without undue interference, he could have sat back and watched the money roll in for decades.

Unfortunately, George ended up killing the goose that laid the golden egg.

How George blew it: the "Swiss watch" school of leadership

George presented himself as an ultra-confident, all-knowing leader. Indeed, he tended to be something of a braggart. But underneath his swaggering façade, he was an insecure, fear-driven person. The more successful his company became, the more terrified he was that somehow it would all be taken away from him.

At the height of his success, George was desperate to make sure his company would always continue exactly as it was, no matter what might happen in the future. His greatest fear was that one member (or several members) of his team would leave, and that he would never be able to replace them with equally good performers.

So what did George do?

He adopted what he called a "Swiss watch" management philosophy. Have you ever heard the expression, "This organization runs like a Swiss watch"? For over a century, Swiss manufacturers have been famous for making mechanical (not digital) watches that are masterpieces of precision engineering, and models of elegance and efficiency. But the point is that in a mechanical watch, every piece is a replaceable unit.

That's what George wanted for his team: he wanted to make sure they were all replaceable. So, he forced every employee to rigidly define his or her own policies and procedures, and then demanded that they mechanistically follow those procedures the same way on every task, in every situation.

Worse yet, George repeatedly told his team that if any of them left, he could easily replace them, and the company would not suffer the slightest hiccup. Why? Because hiring their replacements it would be like swapping one mass-produced, identical part for another. In George's mind, his employees had been reduced to cogs in the workings of a mechanical watch.

Making things worse, George began holding company meetings where he was the only person allowed to talk. He monopolized the conversation, repeating long pointless stories that he'd told many times before. Occasionally if a business decision had to be made, he asked for others' opinions, but he didn't really want to hear them. If any team member dared to speak up – especially to offer a view that differed from his – George's hostile glare made it unmistakable that he deeply resented it.

You will not be surprised to learn what happened. The "Swiss watch" policy, designed to guarantee flawless continuity, created exactly the opposite result. Eventually, the entire team left George's company. A few ex-staff members formed rival companies.

Others opted for employers who treated them with respect -- including respect for their creative talents -- respect for their operating autonomy

-- and respect for them as individual human beings with a right to think for themselves, and a right to have their own opinions.

For three years running, George's company had a 100% employee turnover rate. Somehow his company remained profitable, but its glory days were over. The company's product deteriorated, and its standing in the industry took a huge hit and never recovered.

Whenever George attended an industry conference, his clients and customers said to his face: "How on earth did you let that incredible team go? That was a giant mistake. You should have made them your partners, George."

There are more "Swiss watch" leaders out there than you might think

I never worked for George, but I have certainly experienced my share of mechanistic "Swiss watch" leadership styles, centered on demands for absolute, mindless conformity. I have also experienced the resentment, frustration and reduced productivity that results.

For example, some years ago at the financial services company where I worked, a new President was appointed. He forced every branch of our company to become a mirror image of how he had run his own (highly successful) branch before he was promoted to the top spot.

The President took this policy to ridiculous extremes. Every local team leader had to hold a telephone conference with his team at the same time of morning, every day, covering the same topics. When speaking with clients and potential clients, every individual associate had to use the identical script with the same questions and the same statements in the same order.

Even the physical offices across the country were made into identical units. The new President had them all redecorated so they looked more cookie-cutter than McDonald's restaurants, with the exact same furniture in the same layout, and the same art on the same places on the walls.

Silliest of all, every associate had to use the same brand and color of notebook to write down key information!

All these demands were ludicrous and quickly proved to be counterproductive. Like George's "Swiss watch" management, our new President created resentment, contempt and anger. The leader quickly lost the respect of the led. A year later, he and his top lieutenant lost their jobs, too.

His successor immediately reverted to a style of leadership that valued local autonomy for all of our regional leaders and branch offices. The company became, once again, a vibrant, upbeat, positive place to work.

Unfortunately, these are not isolated cases. There are countless people who believe in the "Swiss watch" school of leadership. But the very characteristics of unity, predictability and 100% conformity that "Swiss watch" leaders see as a strength, are in fact a terrible weakness. People are not interchangeable mechanical parts.

But doesn't "Swiss watch management" succeed at times?

The only place I know of where this kind of leadership works is in the Armed Forces. And, the only reason it works is because each soldier, sailor, flyer or Marine has a well-defined job to perform that requires (and allows) very little creative latitude, except perhaps under extreme wartime conditions.

But even in the chaos of combat, each person in uniform serves in an organization where discipline and instant obedience to orders are crucial to success. That's why every service branch has libraries full of written policies and procedures, covering everything from how to clean your rifle, to how to launch a jet fighter attack from the deck of an aircraft carrier.

Most of life is not the Armed Forces, however! Many leaders (especially men, for some reason) like to use military metaphors in their language, but business is not war. Neither are law, science, art, industry or education. In these fields and most others, military-style conformity is not the ideal to be emulated.

From observation and experience, I can tell you that in most spheres of life, *if you treat human beings like the springs and gears in a watch, your organization will suffer.* And, you will fail as a leader.

Different kinds of people and situations call for different leadership styles

Respect for your team is only the beginning of successful leadership. Recognizing and respecting the *differences between people* is equally crucial. It's also vital to understand that not all *situations, conditions, environments and challenges* are created equal.

That means you need to lead differently for different people in different circumstances. One style of leadership is not enough, but if you only feel comfortable using one style, then your options are severely limited. As the old saying goes, "If the only tool you have is a hammer, you tend to see every problem as a nail."

To take another example, imagine a pro baseball pitcher who had only one pitch – a fastball. No curve ball, no sinker, no slider, no screwball. That pitcher would immediately fail!

To be an effective leader, you need a varied "toolset" of different leadership styles to choose from, and you must be willing and able to use whichever style is appropriate for your team and your situation.

6 classic leadership styles

One of the most popular formulations of basic leadership styles comes from David Goleman, who is best known for inventing the concept of "Emotional Intelligence."

Goleman surveyed more than 3,000 executives and boiled down the results in a study called "Leadership That Gets Results." It was published in the *Harvard Business Review* in the year 2000. (Goleman and a colleague later expanded the article into a couple of books, including one called "Primal Leadership.")

According to Goleman, there are 6 basic leadership styles that work. Briefly, they are: (1) visionary; (2) coaching; (3) affiliative; (4) democratic; (5) pacesetting; and (6) commanding.

In our next chapter we'll delve into these 6 styles in some detail, but first I invite you to consider this stunning statistic...

Studies indicate that up to 54% of leaders use the same style in every situation with every person! These same studies claim only 1% of leaders use 4 or more styles.[15]

Let's suppose for a moment that each style works best for certain people (regardless of situation). Let's further assume that each style works best for roughly an equal-sized slice of the overall population. That means if you're stuck on just one leadership style all the time (out of 6 possible styles), then you're achieving maximum effectiveness for only 1/6th of the population (16%).

A leader must do much better on this score in order to achieve consistent success!

Which leadership style is best? How do you know?

The truth is there is no "right" style of leadership for all people and all situations. And, there is no "right" or "best" style of leadership for you. The "right" style of leadership depends on the answers to 3 sets of questions.

First, what kind of organization are you serving in, and with what authority? Second, what kind of situation are you serving in? Third, what kind of people are you leading?

A good leader carefully considers each of these questions before choosing one of the leadership styles from their toolkit. A <u>great</u> leader

---

15   https://www.kenblanchard.com/Products-Services/SLII

makes that choice instinctively (the "unconsciously competent" level of expertise) and executes that particular style with skill and wisdom.

Specifically...

1) What kind of organization are you serving in, and what is the structure of your leadership role in that organization?

Being promoted to be a general in the U.S. Army is very different from being elected mayor of a small town. And, being appointed to head a tradition-based, precedent-run group (such as a church or court system) is very different from stepping up to lead a group of loosely affiliated activists.

Each type of organization and its associated formal leadership structure requires a different leadership style. The army general can bark commands; the small-town mayor is usually better off building consensus. The high priest or high court justice had better be on firm grounds of precedent for his or her leadership.

Meanwhile, the activist leader usually needs plenty of confidence, vision, originality, personality and charisma -- because in the early days of the movement, there is no formal structure to the followers, and no formal grant of authority. (Gandhi was never elected to any office, but he led the greatest non-violent movement in world history.)

2) What situation are you facing?

What kind of situation are you leading in? Being an army general when you're at war, or under attack, calls for one kind of leadership. Being an army general in peacetime when your main objective is to train thousands of personnel to do their jobs and shape them into an effective force in readiness, requires a totally different style of leadership.

In a similar vein, being the CEO of a sales company that already dominates the market often takes one kind of leadership. Leading that same company through a period of disruptive innovation and retrenchment (especially if the organization loses its grip on the market) often requires a very different style of leadership.

3) What kind(s) of people are you leading?

People make all the difference. If you have a seasoned team of experienced, competent or highly skilled go-getters, that may take one kind of leadership. If you have a team of raw beginners, or people who have basic skills but are not super-experts yet, that frequently takes another – very different -- kind of leadership.

Leading a team whose members have all different levels of experience, may require yet another type of leadership.

In addition, one style of leadership can work great for leading people from the majority culture, but that style may backfire when leading a more culturally, generationally or ethnically diverse team. Finally, a style of leadership that works fine for many men may not work nearly as well for lots of women.

Pat Wadors, the Chief of Human Resources for Linked In, put it brilliantly:

"When we listen and celebrate what is both common and different, we become a wiser, more inclusive, and better organization." [16]

---

16 https://business.linkedin.com/talent-solutions/blog/diversity/2017/how-linkedins-hr-chief-is-changing-the-diversity-conversation-with-belonging

CHAPTER 8

Six dynamic styles of successful leadership

From the Visionary style to the Coaching style, the Pacesetting style and more, there are many "right" ways to lead.

No one is born with innate skills of making the most appropriate choice of leadership style and executing it skillfully and wisely. Both functions require plenty of practice. Eventually, you want to be that "1% leader" who has mastered 4 or 5 of the 6 basic leadership styles.

With this in mind, let's take a closer look at Daniel Goleman's 6 leadership styles. As we discuss these tools, ask yourself: which style or styles am I already using now? If I am going to expand my repertoire, which additional leadership styles might be the most natural fit for me?

For clarity and ease of comparison, we will break down each leadership style into its major components: Key Message, When to Use, How to Use, Strengths, Weaknesses, and Outstanding Examples.

1. The Visionary Leadership Style

The leadership style that creates the most positive impact on followers, says Goleman, is what he calls the Visionary style. "Visionary leaders," he says, "articulate where a group is going, but not how it will get there – setting people free to innovate, experiment, take calculated risks."[17]

KEY MESSAGE: "Come with me! Together we'll go to a fantastic new place, and when we get there it will be glorious."

WHEN TO USE: The Visionary style works best when the team or organization needs a new direction or a jolt of fresh inspiration.

HOW TO USE: Give people an exciting mission. Paint a clear, inspiring picture of the future, linked to a stirring expression of the values and core beliefs that support the mission.

STRENGTHS: The Visionary style inspires and unites people around a shared dream. It also unleashes your followers to be visionaries themselves – to go out there and bring their most creative, inspired efforts to the project.

WEAKNESSES: To be effective, this style of leadership demands an extremely high level of credibility on the part of the leader. That in turn requires a leader to have lots of experience and a strong track record of success. Otherwise, team members will often roll their eyes and dismiss the leader's high-falutin' rhetoric as pretentious. They may even reject the mission as unrealistic and unachievable.

On the other hand, even a visionary with a strong track record of success can be too far ahead of their time. This also works against credibility.

For example, the year after Francis Ford Coppola won an Oscar for directing "The Godfather," he made remarks at the Academy Awards ceremony, forecasting the rise of digital projection, computerized special effects, the end of celluloid as the key medium for cinema, and much more. He was 100% right, but his forecast was so mind-boggling that most of Hollywood didn't understand it.

---

17   From "The Wall Street Journal Guide to Management" by Alan Murray, quoted at https://guides. wsj.com/management/developing-a-leadership-style/how-to-develop-a-leadership-style/

And those who did understand him, still thought he was spouting science-fiction nonsense.

EXAMPLES: Two obvious examples of visionary leaders in politics are Abraham Lincoln giving the Gettysburg Address and John F. Kennedy dedicating America to the Moon mission.

In business, a great example of visionary leadership is Steve Jobs, who said during the 1984 rollout of the first Macintosh computer:

> *"We're gambling on our vision, and we would rather do that than make 'me, too' products. Let some other companies do that. For us, it's always the next dream."*[18]

2. The Coaching Leadership Style

The Coaching style of leadership is often the choice that forges the closest and warmest bond between the leader and the led. This one-on-one style focuses on developing the skills and talents of individuals, showing them how to improve their performance, and helping them reach their potential.

KEY MESSAGE: "Don't worry, you'll get this. Try it this way! Let me show you how, and I'll work closely with you as we practice over and over. I've got your back, and I promise I won't let you fail."

WHEN TO USE: The Coaching style of leadership is most suitable for eager new beginners who are high on enthusiasm but low on skill, and for discouraged neophytes who have tried, failed and lost their self-confidence (these are the first two rungs on the competency ladder). The Coaching style works best, Mr. Goleman writes, "with employees who show initiative and want more professional development."

---

18   https://www.forbes.com/sites/amitchowdhry/2013/10/05/lessons-learned-from-4-steve-jobs-quotes/#1f9389f94f69

HOW TO USE: Have frequent chats with team members. Find out where they're running into trouble and need help. Offer to give them direct, personal instruction and guidance with simple, easy-to-use pointers. Don't be afraid to point out tiny errors and suggest tiny improvements, as long as they are clear and actionable ("Try lifting your right elbow another 2 inches when you swing that tennis racket on your serve").

To ensure that the team member continues to have, or achieves, high motivation and strong loyalty to the organization, connect their personal goals and dreams with the goals of the team or the company.

STRENGTH: The great strength of the Coaching style of leadership is that it creates a reassuring impact for the follower. It also promotes powerful emotional bonding of the "coach" and the "student" (i.e., a strong "vertical" connection between the leader and the led).

WEAKNESS: When the leader focuses almost exclusively on individual step-by-step performance today, it can result in underemphasis on achieving group goals tomorrow. In addition, team members who need – and receive – less personal attention from the leader, can feel slighted, which may create jealousy or resentment.

The Coaching style can backfire if team members perceive it as a form of micromanaging, or as a form of implicit criticism which undermines the follower's self-confidence.

Finally, the Coaching style depends on personal rapport between leader and led. This can be challenging to achieve if they are very different ages, belong to different races, or come from very different cultures or backgrounds.

EXAMPLES: The natural place to find high-visibility examples of the Coaching style in action is among actual coaches in professional and college sports. My personal favorite Coaching style leader is Dawn Staley, head coach of the Gamecocks women's basketball team at the University of South Carolina. A Hall of Fame member, Staley is also three-time Olympic Gold medalist, ABL pro player, and winner of all 3 major national Coach of the Year awards in a single year.

She explains her winning philosophy of coaching this way:

> *"My goal is always to decrease the amount of time it takes for us to make a connection, because that's where it all starts. If there were ever a secret to being a great coach, that's it: the connection. I need to have a personal relationship with each player. Just like they do, I have to be invested. Something other than basketball has to draw me to them. Basketball is the immediate common ground between us, of course, but I'm talking about a personal level. I like to have something more."* [19]

3. The Affiliative Leadership Style

If the Coaching style is about "vertical" one-to-one relationships between the leader and the led, the Affiliative style of leadership is about "horizontal" one-to-many relationships between and among different team members.

The leader largely stays in the background (or at least, tries to remain above the fray). The leader's goal is to encourage team members to "play nice together," to respect and value their fellow team members, to embrace teamwork, to take pride in group achievements rather than individual wins, and to learn to love the atmosphere of harmony and mutual support that can result.

KEY MESSAGE: "People come first. We're far stronger together than working apart or at cross-purposes. Putting the whole group first is

---

19   https://www.theplayerstribune.com/en-us/articles/dawn-staley-south-carolina-coach

the best way to achieve the success that we all want. Let's all recognize the value that each of us brings to this team, and help each other succeed."

WHEN TO USE: The ideal time for the Affiliative style of leadership is when the leader needs to heal a broken team spirit, or to create a team ethic that has been lost to destructive levels of competition, jealousy, backbiting, mistrust, criticism and backstabbing.

HOW TO USE: Affiliative leaders may talk to individual team members, but their focus is on speaking to the team as a whole. When they do talk, they lead with praise, appreciation and encouragement. (As one Affiliative leader explained, "The commodity that is most lacking in this world is encouragement.")

Praise can be a powerful motivator, but how you give praise is vitally important. A successful Affiliative leader praises the whole team as a group, more than they praise individuals. Or, when they must single out individuals for praise, they focus on multiple team members, or perhaps even praise all of them, each in their turn. They never praise just one or two team members, because in a team where mutual bitterness has become a fact of life, selective praise is too easily perceived as a slight against all those who were not mentioned.

The flip side of the coin is great reserve when it comes to saying anything that might be perceived as negative. Affiliative leaders are extremely cautious and sparing about giving criticism. Rather than bluntly saying, "You made a mistake, fix it" they tend to give constructive criticism: "Well, that didn't work out as well as we'd hoped, did it? Next time, why don't we try XYZ instead?"

If Affiliative leaders must criticize, they lean heavily on the "sandwich technique," where one criticism is gently "sandwiched" between two compliments:

> *"Joe, I love how you got that report in*
> *early last week; it gave me extra time*
> *to absorb your findings.*

*"I might have ideally hoped for a lit-
tle more specificity in the section on
Vendor Costs -- that's easily fixed.*

*"And by the way, thanks for follow-
ing our format starting with a one-
page Executive Summary. That makes
it much easier for me to absorb all
the data."*

The group-centric focus of Affiliative leadership can be extended to rewards and compensation, too. Rather than handing out individual merit awards or individual bonuses, the group can work toward winning a Team of the Month Plaque and/or a team bonus (such as a celebratory team dinner at a nice restaurant, etc.).

STRENGTHS: The great strength of the Affiliative style is that it cre-ates harmony between team members that may have been lacking before. This can result in team members who go out of their way to support, assist, educate and cover for each other. This in turn can lead to phenomenal performance and achievement.

WEAKNESS: Affiliative leadership may frustrate more-experienced peers or highly competitive individuals who are eager to show what they can do as a solo performer. This kind of team member craves individual recognition, and may resent spending one minute of their "spare time" covering for anyone else, or playing mentor to any-one else.

Affiliative leadership comes with another potential weakness. Group rewards and recognition, where lagging performers get equal ben-efits to superstars, can be destructive to morale. In a way, they are like group punishments, where everyone pays for the sins of a few individuals. Neither is really fair, especially if you have the American super-individualist ethic.

Finally, Affiliative leadership is so averse to criticism that it can slide into refusing to hold people to any standards whatsoever. This lack of accountability can lead to chronic underperformance. As Goleman put it, "Employees may perceive that mediocrity is tolerated."

EXAMPLES: Goleman's most frequently cited example of Affiliative style leadership is New York Yankees manager Joe Torre, especially during the team's World Series winning year of 1999.

But examples of this nurturing, harmonizing style can be found everywhere. Think of a hospital where the nursing staff begins the year in mutual hostility and ends in harmony. Or consider a symphony orchestra where the musicians start off as insanely jealous of "who gets paid more" and "who gets the most solos," but they end up by declaring, "We are so proud of our Grammy Awards, and of each other."

4. The Democratic Leadership Style

In the Democratic style of leadership, the leader does a lot of consulting. He or she asks team members to share their views on big questions and takes those views into account, or at least gives them their due weight in any decision.

Team members feel valued and respected, and they feel encouraged to bring their full strengths to the enterprise, not just sticking to their spot on the organization chart or within the confines of their narrowly defined job description.

KEY MESSAGE: "What do you think? We have some interesting alternatives here and it might be useful to have an open, free discussion of the pros and cons of each one. I'd like to hear each of your views. Please feel free to speak up, no matter how out of left field, and even if you're the only one who feels that way. Let's all keep in mind, sometimes the lone voice of dissent turns out to be the person with the right answer. In this organization, we believe that a great idea can come from anyone at any time."

WHEN TO USE: Goleman suggests that the best time to use the Democratic style is when the future is unclear and a new path forward must be chosen. But there are other excellent times to use this approach. For example, when you're leading a team of genuine superstars (Lincoln's "Team of Rivals" cabinet is an obvious example). Another time when the Democratic leadership style makes sense is when your organization is moving into new, uncharted territory where past experience may not provide a reliable guide to future prospects and conditions.

HOW TO USE: Taking a formal vote is fine, of course, but consulting your team members can involve many other "polling techniques." For example, it can mean making it a frequent habit to casually buttonhole somebody in the hallway to get their reaction to an idea, or ask for their thoughts on a problem. Consulting your team can also mean having an "open door policy" where every person is encouraged to make an appointment or just drop in to chat informally with the leader and share their thoughts. Democratic leadership can be expressed by something as simple as a suggestion box -- sometimes with a monetary reward promised if a suggestion is adopted. It doesn't matter if any brilliant suggestions are ever made are not. The point is, if the team or the organization knows their views are welcome, considered and may be acted upon, it boosts morale and loyalty across the board.

In an actual meeting with team members seated around the table (or logging into Zoom), the Democratic style can simply be a vigorous, wide-ranging, open-ended conversation. It can even be a classic brainstorming session.

STRENGTHS: One major value of this style is its ability to create consensus and get everyone's buy-in, or at least their support, based on the fact that their opinions were heard and duly considered.

Another strength of the Democratic leadership style is that it leverages the full skill set and knowledge of every member of the team. Group discussion can tap into the collective wisdom of the team, which sometimes proves better than the combined sum of individual knowledge. Team members who have a genuine back-and-forth dialog can build on each other's points and insights.

WEAKNESS: One potential drawback of the Democratic leadership style is that it can lead to stalemate, resulting in indecision. That may be perfectly fine under routine conditions, because the organization can usually afford to wait until a clear-cut set of indicators shows which path is unquestionably correct. But in a crisis that demands "action and action now," such paralysis can be deadly.

Another potential drawback of this style of leadership is that it tends to put a premium on the views of those who speak up loudest, most often and with the greatest sense of self-confidence – regardless of whether their self-confidence is justified or not. Leaders who solicit input from their team need to be extremely careful about separating style from substance.

EXAMPLES: One of the most dramatic examples of the Democratic leadership style in action was a high-level strategy session that President Harry Truman had with his top military and War Department staff to discuss possible plans to invade the Japanese home islands in mid-1945. Each of the generals and admirals had their say. They all talked in terms of conventional amphibious invasion, supported by naval and aerial assault. (The atomic bomb was in an advanced stage of development at this point, but had not been tested and proven yet.)

As the meeting seemed to be drawing to a close, Truman turned to the Assistant Secretary for War, John J. McCloy. He said, "McCloy, what about you? We don't end the meeting until everyone has been heard from." McCloy urged Truman to use the A-bomb. It was the first time that the weapon had been discussed in a U.S. military strategy session. And, as Truman later said, it ended the war.

In the world of big business, a prominent believer in the "let every voice be heard" style of Democratic leadership was Alfred P. Sloan, Chairman of General Motors from the 1930s through the 1950s.

Sloan firmly believed that if his team had a deep understanding of an issue, they would naturally evolve differing points of view about it. Whenever there was 100% consensus, he suspected they had a superficial acquaintance with the topic, or they were simply missing something. For this reason, Sloan once closed a meeting of his top executives by saying:

> *"I take it we are all in complete agreement on the decision here. Then, I propose we postpone further discussion of this matter until the next meeting to give ourselves time to develop disagreement and perhaps gain some understanding of what the decision is all about."*[20]

5. The Pacesetting Leadership Style

The Pacesetting style of leadership is one that Daniel Goleman has characterized as having a high potential for great results, but an equally high potential for negative results if misused or overused. For this reason, and because it's far easier to misuse this style than to get it right, quite a few experts urge leaders to avoid using it altogether.

Pacesetting leadership is about setting the bar high for great performance. The Pacesetting leader does not ask, he demands that his team do the impossible – and he demands that the team achieve those results on an "impossible" or "totally unreasonable" timetable or budget.

It's called "Pacesetting" because the leader is running out front, routinely working the 80-hour or 100-hour weeks themselves that they ask everyone else to emulate. They become the inspiring example, or in some cases, the unhealthy example, of what the team should do.

---

20   Quoted in Peter F. Drucker's classic book "The Effective Executive."

KEY MESSAGE: "Do as I do – right now! Look, team, our challenge isn't taking any weekends off and it's not taking any vacations. Neither are we. If we want to achieve stunningly great results, we have no choice but to make 'insanely huge' efforts and sacrifices. Trust me, this crazy level of dedication is how we can bring out the best in ourselves. When we pull off the big win, it will all have been worth it."

WHEN TO USE: The most apt time to pull this gun out of the holster is when a crash program is necessary to achieve a vitally important goal on an emergency basis. This style of leadership probably works best when the team is already on the same page as the leader – meaning, they are both super-motivated and ultra-competent.

HOW TO USE: To be an effective Pacesetting leader, above all lead by example. This is the most important way that you set the standard for your team to live up to. If you want team members to show up at 6 a.m. and go home at midnight (or maybe sleep in the office), then you do it first. If you want the team to give up their personal lives to dedicate themselves wholly to the mission, you do it first.

Next, be vocal in stating what you expect: excellence in a hurry. Amazing results. Challenge your team by urging them, "Come on, blow my mind!" (Note: the team has to admire the Pacesetting leader enough to want to blow his or her mind in the first place, or this appeal won't work).

A dash of Visionary leadership is pretty much mandatory here. Team members only make "insane" sacrifices for the mission when they have a clear, inspiring mental picture of the amazingly great thing the organization is seeking to achieve.

Finally, Pacesetting leadership is the opposite of micromanagement. It declares the goal, then gets out of the way. It gives team members complete freedom to do whatever they believe is necessary to deliver superb results. In many cases, the team (or each individual member) works independently of top management; they only meet every week or every month to give updates.

STRENGTHS: The great strength of Pacesetting leadership is that it provides the fuel of inspiration that prods a team to reach for the stars and achieve peak performance. This creates a culture of "whatever it takes" – something that countless companies talk about, but almost none actually believe in, want, attempt, or achieve.

WEAKNESSES: Obviously, Pacesetting can promote workaholism, especially if it is permanently used as the organization's main or sole style of leadership. Pacesetting can exact very high costs in terms of health, happiness and family relationships. Work-life balance? Forget it. And, Pacesetting "followership" can ea**sily** lead to fatigue and burnout, no matter how dedicated and motivated team members might be.

According to Goleman, the Pacesetting style should be used only on occasion. It should not be relied upon as the leader's standard, everyday, go-to style. If for no other reason, setting one "impossible" goal after another can backfire, crashing company morale and leading people to feel a pervasive sense of hopelessness and failure. "Our data shows that, more often than not, pacesetting poisons the climate," Goleman concluded.[21]

EXAMPLES: An outstanding positive example of Pacesetting leadership can be found in the response of a major global pharmaceutical company to the H1N1 flu pandemic of 2009. Executives and factory workers alike pitched in on a 24-hour basis, 6 days a week, to run the vaccine production and packaging lines. The mission was to save lives. Each carton of medical vials was shipped out as soon as it came off the line. Federal marshals literally grabbed the boxes of ready-to-use vaccine and ran to load them on trucks, which then raced to the airport. This red-alert operation went on for month after month.

"In a pandemic, people rise to the occasion and do extraordinary things," said one of the company's top executive leaders, who was right there with the rest of the team. "They work incredible hours

---

21   https://guides.wsj.com/management/developing-a-leadership-style/
how-to-develop-a-leadership-style/

and make personal sacrifices because it is the 'right thing to do.'" This award-winning executive also recalled: "The pandemic emergency brought everyone together and people went the extra mile. Everyone felt great to be part of that effort. We all celebrated being able to make a difference."

A negative example of the Pacesetting leadership style is the world-famous, super-innovative auto manufacturing executive who asked his team to pull off an incredible engineering feat in a matter of weeks. This was a goal that would ordinarily be expected to take months, if not years.

"That's impossible," said the engineers.

The executive replied: "If I held a gun to your head, and said I would pull the trigger if you failed to meet the deadline...you know something? I'll bet you guys would find a way to meet the deadline. I want you to imagine that this is exactly what you're facing. Do it or get your brains blown out."

As it turned out, the leader was right. The "impossible" goal could be achieved by going to that level of dire emergency effort. Somehow, the engineering team managed to pull off a miracle and meet the deadline.

But at what cost to morale and company loyalty? At what cost to health and happiness? Sometimes even when you win, you lose – and in my mind, this was one of those times.

6. The Commanding Leadership Style

This Commanding style of leadership is pure authoritarianism or (ideally) a form of "benevolent dictatorship." That is not necessarily a negative. Remember that back in Ancient Rome, where the title and office of Dictator was invented 2,000 years ago, dictatorship was an honorable and popular institution. (But it was a short-term job, not for life, and it did not involve god-like authority over all things).

Command-style leadership in today's world is based on the leader exercising absolute authority, and the team giving absolute obedience. This makes the Commanding leadership style potentially extremely powerful and effective.

It also makes this style of leadership potentially extremely dangerous for that very same reason. (As the aphorism states, "Power corrupts; and absolute power corrupts absolutely").

Used rightly and under the appropriate circumstances, Commanding leadership can save the day and can achieve wonderful, amazing things. Misused or abused, it can wreck careers, lives, products, and companies.

KEY MESSAGE: "I'm in charge, so do as I say -- period. This isn't a democracy; at the moment I don't really care what you think. I have the power to give orders here because I've proven that I have the ability and knowledge to lead this outfit to victory. Maybe I'll share my strategy with you, if I think it will make you more effective in the field. But maybe I won't share my strategy with you, because I can't afford to tip my hand to the enemy or to the competition. In that case, you'll simply have to go forward on blind faith and obedience. My track record of success, and the importance of the goal we seek -- or the severity of the threat we face -- justifies my claim to this absolute authority."

WHEN TO USE: The best time for employing Command-style leadership is in a crisis, or when there is a huge, urgent opportunity. But remember, even the U.S. Army tends to use a somewhat more relaxed form of discipline in peacetime. (And, the Army ultimately reports to civilian control, which is democratically elected).

HOW TO USE: The leader must issue clear orders and decisive directions. Expect and demand full and instant compliance. If you don't get it, discipline people. If you still don't get it, fire them. But until you have to fire them, and even after you fire them, treat them with respect. (There is a phrase for commanders who abuse and bully their troops. They are called bullies and abusers).

STRENGTHS: A confident leader who uses Command-style leadership can be inspiring and give courage and confidence to her followers. She does much more than bark orders. She provides thoughtful direction, a clear and well-organized structure, and the stability of a rigid command hierarchy. These are extremely valuable commodities, especially in an emergency, and they should not be overlooked when considering this leadership style.

WEAKNESSES: Command-style leadership, exercised in a culture that is accustomed to democracy and egalitarianism, can provoke resent-ment, create foot-dragging, and lead to passive or active resistance.

In addition, this is a more demanding style of leadership to execute well than it may appear. You just give orders, right? And if anyone disagrees, you just mow them down, yes? Actually, no.

The stereotype about Command-style leadership is that it involves screaming at people, calling them names and otherwise abusing your followers or team. This is what very bad Commanding leaders do, but it's not something great Commanding leaders would ever dream of.

EXAMPLES: A superb example of positive and successful Commanding-style leadership, used for the most beneficial of reasons and only in an urgent situation, is found in the career of Peter J. Velardi, the CEO of Vanity Fair – America's largest lingerie manufacturer.

At a certain point, Peter realized there was a huge sales opportunity for the company if it could create a V-back bra in a matter of months, and rush it into stores before a certain new fashion wave from Europe arrived in the U.S. market.

Peter ordered the company's merchandise manager – a man named John -- to have their designers modify an existing new bra that had been developed with a different back closure. John protested "We can't possibly do that," and gave Peter one argument after another why his decision could not be carried out.

After several rounds of this dispute, Peter put his foot down. He said quietly but firmly, "John, this is an order. I need you to change these bras to V-back, so you're going to do it, and you're not going to say no because it's going to be done."

John reluctantly agreed. But 15 minutes later, he came back to resume the argument again!

"John," Peter said in a voice that brooked no resistance, "these bras *will* be V-back. We *will* introduce them in the new market, and we *will* have the money for delivery in 30 days, like we always do with every new product."

At last, John caved in and followed Peter's orders. The company's V-back bra was introduced in the U.S. almost a year before the competition had a chance to catch up. It became by far the bestselling garment that Vanity Fair ever made.

But this triumph only happened because Peter Velardi pulled rank and exercised "dictatorial" power -- with notable restraint, and for the best of reasons.[22]

Negative examples of "Commanding style leadership gone wrong" are too numerous to count. The U.S. business grapevine is overrun with tales of frothing-at-the-mouth, red-faced Silicon Valley CEOs yelling at their underlings and hurling belittling insults at their team.

Personally, I'm still trying to figure out what class it is at Harvard Business School where they teach future CEOs that degrading people is a great way to motivate your team and to bring out their best. So far as I know, there is no such class – and I'm pretty sure there never will be.

Successful leadership is about more than leadership style. It's about people and how we relate to them

The 6 styles of leadership identified by Daniel Goleman and outlined above are terrific ways to think about leadership, especially in a variety of situations and with a variety of people who need to be led.

---

22   From "45 Years in Ladies' Panties" by Peter J. Velardi and Marcus Webb, 2018. Bellissimo Angelina Publications.

At the same time, these 6 styles represent just a few of the many ways that leadership has been defined, categorized and classified. There are scores of other models, some of them quite good, and these days many such models are supported by reams of studies and scientific data.

But a theory is just that, a theory -- until you put into practice. And to do that, you need a team to lead.

Our next chapter will look at today's workforce and how an effective leader embraces them in all their wonderful diversity – not only with different leadership styles, but also with customized techniques and tactics -- depending on the people, the organization and the situation.

As we'll see, Tomorrow's Leader is a citizen of the world, because he or she understands and anticipates the world of tomorrow. Front and center is the evolving global population that drives an evolving customer base, an evolving pool of potential team members, and – in a successful organization -- an evolving corporate culture.

6 Dynamic Styles of Leadership: there's a style for every team and situation

Leadership Style	VISIONARY	COACHING	AFFILIATIVE	DEMOCRATIC	PACESETTING	COMMANDING
What the leader DOES	Leader articulates clear vision of where the group is going and why it's good	Leader provides one- on-one skill development for each team member	Leader encourages all team members to support each other as a group	Leader consults team members constantly, genuinely respects & considers their views	Leaders sets super- high goals & aggressive deadlines; provides personal example of commitment	Leaders exercise sole authority to decide the goal and strategy; expect followers to obey orders
What the leader SAYS	"Come with me! When we get there, here's why it will be great"	"I've got your back. I'll work closely with you as we practice over and over"	"We're strongest when we help each other succeed. Take pride in our group."	"What do you think? Everyone's point of view is important to this organization"	"Our goal is so important that it demands total dedication & sacrifices from us all"	"I'm in charge because I know what I'm doing, so do what I say and we'll win"
WHEN to use	When team needs a brand-new direction, a clearer sense of direction, or a jolt of fresh inspiration	When team members are new or need to improve their skills	When teams have lost trust in each other or when intra-team competition has become destructive	When future path is unclear; when leader wants to bond with team as a group, as well as one-on-one	Best used in an emergency when a crash program is needed to achieve a vitally important goal	When a dangerous crisis occurs or a huge, urgent opportunity arises
HOW to use	Paint clear, inspiring picture of the goal, linked to a stirring expression of team's values and core beliefs	Make a personal connection with team members, provide simple pointers and demonstrations	Speak more to the group than to individuals; focus on praise, appreciation and encouragement	Take a formal vote, or just chat with as many team members as possible (solo or as a group), do more listening than talking	Lead by example: set the pace & the standard, and (vocally) set expectation	Give clear orders and decisive directions; enforce discipline to ensure obedience in the ranks
Strengths	Unites people around a shared dream, excites and unleashes followers to be creative	Reassures followers, creates powerful personal bond between leader and led	Creates harmony among the team, leading to strong mutual support and cooperation	Leverages "wisdom of crowds"; gets everyone's buy-in if they feel they've been heard fairly	Provides inspiration and motivation for team members to "reach for the stars"	Can instill courage and confidence, get quick results, and provide stable, well-organized structure
Drawbacks	Leader must be eloquent & credible; can't be too far ahead of their time	Can seem like micromanaging; focus on individual needs can lose sight of group's overall goal	May frustrate "stars" who desire solo achievement; may fail to voice needed criticism or correction	Requiring 100% consensus can create stalemate; loudest team members may have undue influence	Often requires super competent, motivated team members; can lead to rapid burnout	Can create a culture clash, leading to resentment or even rebellion or desertion
Examples	Elon Musk (Tesla), Steve Jobs (Apple), Queen Elizabeth I, Martin Luther King Jr.	John Wooden (UCLA Coach), Olympics coach Sam Mussabini (immortalized in the Oscar-winning film "Chariots of Fire")	Sara Blakely (Spanx), Herb Kelleher (Southwest Airlines) , Richard Branson (Virgin) , Zack Mayo in "An Officer and a Gentleman" learns to become this kind of leader	Eleanor Roosevelt, Google's Larry Page, Nelson Mandela, Abraham Lincoln	Michael Jordan, Jack Welch (GE), Jeff Bezos (Amazon), Ariana Huffington (Huffington Post)	Steve Jobs (Apple), General George S. Patton, Jr.; Margaret Thatcher; Henry Ford (Ford Motor); Sgt. Foley in "An Officer and a Gentleman"

CHAPTER 9

You will meet many different personalities on your path to successful leadership

In today's highly diverse society and fast-changing economy, the best leaders adapt to the people they lead.

I can truthfully say that I learned one of my most valuable lessons in leadership from a dormant volcano. Specifically, Haleakalā on the island of Maui, in Hawaii.

You might think that in that stunningly beautiful surrounding, with magnificent views everywhere you look, the lesson would be inspiring, thrilling and uplifting.

It was pretty close to the opposite.

By now probably millions of people are familiar with the famous Haleakala bike ride, one of the Aloha State's most popular attractions. Several companies offer this experience, but each provides pretty much the same package. A van comes to your hotel and picks up your group at 5 a.m., driving you 10,000 feet up to the top of mountain. Reaching the peak takes 45 minutes.

During the ride, your guides share fun stories, ancient legends, and local culture (Haleakalā, they explain, means "House of the Sun"). They also describe the geography, flowers and trees that you'll be seeing, and give you a brief safety lecture.

Your van arrives at the top, just before sunrise. You get out next to the mountaintop observatory and see the stars overhead. You witness a breathtaking sunrise and see the Pacific stretching out to the horizon. What a sight!

Then you pile back into the van for a quick ride to your launch point, which is back down around the 6,000-foot level. (Any higher and most people have trouble breathing).

You disembark a second time. By now you are super-excited and raring to go. The guides provide bicycles, helmets, gloves, and whatever gear you need.

Then you're off – freewheeling 30 miles down the mountain, getting one eye-popping view after another every time you zip around a bend. There's a quick stop for lunch, and then you're back on the road. By mid-afternoon you're back at the van pickup point, and you've got a high that lasts three days.

Depending on speed, your bike ride from the launch point back down to sea level can take anywhere from two to four hours, or even five hours if you choose a really leisurely pace.

Since your bike is coasting downhill, you don't have to work at pedaling. You can peddle as much or as little as you like, or simply coast effortlessly. The roads are smooth and well-paved, and traffic is minimal. The road is yours and you can pretty much take charge of your destiny.

That's what I expected, anyway. I'm a somewhat athletic person, and I was excitedly looking forward to what I thought would be one of the great thrills of my lifetime.

Imagine a blazing race down the face of Haleakalā! I saw myself with the wind in my face! My bike careening through the miles at a blistering pace! Nothing to hold me back! Just sky, sun, tropical breezes and limitless speed!

I could not wait for that exhilarating sense of freedom, a jolt of pure freedom that you can't get anyplace else (short of a high-performance jet plane, perhaps).

To say that my expectations were dashed would be a vast understatement.

It turned out that our tour company had one strict rule: everybody in the group must stay together, and the pace is set by the slowest, least proficient biker in the group.

In other words, we kept our brakes clamped down hard all day. We inched down the mountain so slowly that my second-biggest challenge was not to lose the minimum speed required to remain upright.

My _biggest_ challenge was not to scream with frustration. I wanted to yell at the tour guides:

> *"What is the matter with you people? Don't you realize you're killing this entire experience? Are you seriously going to make me creep down this mountain like an old lady, when I could be soaring like an eagle? I don't care how pretty the scenery is, I want to MOVE!"*

I'm pretty sure that by the time we reached the bottom of the mountain, my blood pressure had gone up 20 or 30 points from sheer stress, anger and frustration.

I rate this a massive failure of leadership, and an equally massive failure in customer service, on the part of the Maui bike tour company. They had been around for decades and no doubt have many happy customers, but I suspect they have also had plenty of customers like me whose biggest emotion at the end was not joy, but regret for a frustrating, wasted day.

The mystifying part of this whole story is how easy it would have been for the company to serve everyone. All they had to do was divide us into three groups – the slow, the moderate, and the fast – each accompanied by a guide. Then everyone could have gone at the pace they liked, and enjoyed the day much more.

I notice that these days, the original company offering this experience now has several competitors, including one or two that offer "set your own pace" biking experiences down the face of Maui. If the original company had done that first, they could have avoided giving competitors an opening. They could have kept a larger share of the business for themselves, and generated larger annual profits.

There is a huge lesson here for leadership that applies to any company, group or organization.

People are different, and it's a giant mistake to treat them all the same (and to attempt to lead them all the same way)

My frustrating day on Maui taught me, in an unforgettable way, how counterproductive it can be to lump all team members into the same group and treat everyone with cookie-cutter conformity.

The essence of human nature is our individuality. Each of us is as unique as our thumbprint. We all have different goals, values, and motivations. We have different work styles. We certainly prefer different paces and different types of working environments.

Let me share a counter-story that shows what savvy leadership looks like, when it comes to dealing with very different kinds of personalities.

How to get a dehydrated NFL linebacker to drink enough water during a pro football game

Dr. Jim Payne had two simultaneous careers, and they were a highly unlikely combination. On the one hand, he was a professor of special education at the University of Virginia and later, at the University of Mississippi.

But when Dr. Payne wasn't teaching classes, he was a highly successful corporate consultant who specialized in solving tough motivational and management problems for large, famous companies.

As I recall one story told by Dr. Payne, many years ago he was hired by the (then) Washington Redskins to help that team get better performance out of its defensive and offensive linemen. These are the hulking 300-pound monsters who love to tear up the turf and run over their opponents like a Mac Truck squashing Bambi.

If that kind of language seems offensive to you, then you are showing a *"people are all the same (or should be)"* bias right now. There may be exceptions, but 99% of linebackers love that kind of talk. They get excited thinking of themselves as unstoppable warriors -- as the fiercest, most aggressive, most testosterone-raging animals in the jungle.

In fact, the more they see themselves this way, the better they play, and Jim Payne had statistics to prove it.

But he saw problems with the way the Redskins coaching staff was treating these players. Several of these problems, and his creative solutions, are outlined in one of his many books.[23] But in a lecture I once heard him give, he told a story that I've never forgotten.

The linebackers were playing their hearts out and sweating like crazy during every game, so naturally they were getting dehydrated. But they flat-out refused to drink enough water.

Nothing seemed to help. The coaching staff tried switching from water to Gatorade. They tried other sports drinks. They tried sugary colas. They tried milkshakes. The linemen refused to drink anything.

As a result, their physical strength declined measurably as each game progressed. Yards were lost, points were lost, games were lost. Management was going crazy.

---

23   Dr. James S. Payne, "PeopleWise: Brain to Brain." Copyright 2004. Sterlinghouse Publisher, Inc.

"Will you guys *please* drink more water?" the team physician used to beg at practices. No dice.

Dr. Payne quickly saw the problem and fixed it. The water was brought to linemen on the sidelines by a wimpy-looking guy who carried a big round tray of tiny paper cups filled with H20, like the kind of disposable cups you see at a medical infirmary. The linemen were supposed to drink as many cups as they wanted, then put the empties back on the tray for the server to neatly dispose of.

The problem is, the linemen hated this "weakling" serving style. They hated the oval tray, which to them looked like something out of a snooty hotel's dining salon. They hated the tiny paper cups, which they were forced to hold daintily between their fingers, and take tiny sips from, in order to drink. (The linemen who did drink from the tiny paper cups refused to put them back on the tray, but crushed them and threw them on the ground as hard as they could.)

Dr. Payne got rid of the tray, the tiny paper cups and the wimpy server. He put in new hydration system in place where linemen could get a BLAST of water from a hose! They would stand by the bench and some tough-looking guy would take the hose and shoot water into their mouths. Then the server would hose them down from head to toe for good measure.

The linemen loved it! Now every time they got a drink of water, they felt like invincible Army tanks. They felt like unstoppable machines with clanking tread and mobile cannon, ready to destroy the opposition. Suddenly the linemen were taking a blast of water every 10 minutes and they were physically stronger as a result. Team performance improved. Problem solved.

Would this approach work for, say, the caregivers at a hospice? Almost certainly not.

But that's the point: different strokes for different folks. Not just different speeds when you bike down the mountain, but different styles of getting basic resources (like water). And different rewards for great performance. And different ways of leaders interacting with followers.

So let's take a quick look at just a few of the various leadership factors that can and should be customized for different kinds of people – like the people on your team.

But regardless of specifics, please remember the basic principle. People are different and a successful leader takes those differences into account, providing a different brand, style or method of leadership depending on the personalities she's dealing with.

Over-leading, under-leading, and finding the "just right" amount of interaction for each team member

All leaders, whether they realize it or not, face the question of "how much" leadership their team requires, and that applies to each individual member as well.

Over-leading might be described as providing a micro-managing, in-your-face "coaching" style of leadership to someone who doesn't need it. They are perfectly competent to get the job done; you just have to tell them what the goal and the deadline are, and they will take care of the rest. If they have a problem, they'll come to you on their own initiative.

Under-leading, naturally, is the opposite. It's setting team members adrift at sea with no navigational help from the leader, when what they need is someone to check in with them fairly often and evaluate their performance step by step – maybe day by day, or in extreme cases, hour by hour. If they don't get that kind of frequent, detailed feedback (and instruction), they're at sea without a paddle or compass.

The point is, under-leading and over-leading are not fixed amounts of leading. They are a mismatch of "how much leading you give" in the context of "how much leading does your team (or an individual member) happen to need." The same amount of active, hands-on leadership could be under-leading for neophyte Sam Smith, but over-leading for experienced, capable Betty Brown.

Under-leading risks failures and loss of confidence by the team member, who may lose all enthusiasm for the project or the organization. They are also likely to suffer diminished confidence in the leader who failed to help them when they needed it.

Over-leading carries its own risks. No one likes to be micro-managed, and team members can resent the implied lack of faith on the part of a leader who coaches when they should focus on setting the overarching goals.

How can you tell what's the right amount of leadership to provide to different teams and people? Start by giving them small tasks to perform on their own and see how they do. If they succeed, give them more responsibility. If they run into trouble, give them more help the next time.

Another obvious way to decide how much leadership to provide is – ask your team! There is no rule against saying, "How much do you need me to work with you on this? Are you fine handling it on your own, or would you rather that I check in more frequently?" Always make it clear that there is no penalty or stigma to asking questions or requesting more help from the leader.

By the way, as your team members climb the steps of the competency ladder (see Chapter Two), they will progressively require less hands-on management and less close supervision by the leader.

Today's workforce includes Baby Boomers, Generations X and Y, and Millennials...it includes men and women...and it includes culturally and ethnically diverse team members

To a certain kind of leader, there is only one "right" kind of leadership and all team members must conform to it.

I've seen offices where everyone is required to wear a jacket and tie, or a dress or suit, and is required to show up at 8:00 a.m., required take 30 minutes for lunch (from 12:00 sharp to 12:30) and go home on the dot at 4:30 p.m. During the day the performance of each team member is as regimented as their clothing and calendar.

That is certainly an option for leaders, but anyone who make this choice is guaranteed to pay for it in terms of sub-optimal performance. There are millions of great team members who refuse to be "led" (or controlled) this way. If they join such a straitjacketed team at all, they're likely to be looking for a quick exit.

McKinsey, the famed consulting company, released a report called *Diversity Matters* in 2015.[24] Based on analyzing extensive data sets from 366 public companies across a wide range of industries, McKinsey noted the following:

- Companies in the top quartile for racial and ethnic diversity are 35 percent more likely to have financial returns above their respective national industry medians.

- Companies in the top quartile for gender diversity are 15 percent more likely to have financial returns above their respective national industry medians.

Why do diverse teams generate better financial returns? Because they perform better. This includes multi-disciplinary teams, too, where people with different skill sets and kinds of expertise all work together.

Often, diverse teams bring a wide variety of strengths, education, experiences and thinking styles to the table. Once team members learn to constructively combine their varied views and methods, they can come up with better solutions to problems.

---

24   https://www.mckinsey.com/business-functions/organization/our-insights/why-diversity-matters#

Providing different kinds of leadership to different kinds of team members

Learning how to provide diverse leadership to diverse teams and organizations can easily be a lifelong study. There is a great deal to say about it; new learning and fresh insights arrive on a daily basis.

Here, let me just outline a few very basic pointers that may help you get your thinking moving in a direction of greater sensitivity to today's multicultural, multi-chronological and increasingly "multi-gendered" society, and the implications of these factors for successful leadership.

Of necessity, what follows includes some very large-scale generalizations and even oversimplifications. It should be noted that there will always be many exceptions to every trend, and infinite variations on every average or composite figure.

Leading by age group: why Baby Boomers and Millennials often respond to different leadership styles

When it comes to leading an age-diverse workforce, keep in mind that the "typical" Baby Boomer (born 1946-1964) tends to be more comfortable (than younger peers) in more of a highly structured, top-down, chain of command structure.

Perhaps that's because Boomers are more willing to take things on faith. If management says it, that doesn't necessarily mean it's true -- but it does mean that is the policy, so salute the flag and get moving.

Having given this kind of loyalty to a company or organization, Boomers tend to stay longer with a single team. They are not as prone to job-hopping as younger workers may be.

Which of the six leadership styles work best for Boomers? All of them — depending on the situation, the goal, the company, and the individual personalities involved. But Boomers are more likely than other age cohorts to enjoy Affiliative leadership styles. Why?

Because they intend to stay longer in one place and develop long-term work relationships.

Boomers are also more open to Visionary leadership styles, because of their love of idealism. They are more open to Commanding leadership styles because of their comfort with well-defined, top-down hierarchies. Again, all of this is relative compared to younger generations.

For younger generations (and again, this is a very broad generalization), it's understood that the modern economy changes quickly, and that individual company priorities change just as fast. Therefore, the logic of the "typical" Millennial is:

"If my job could be eliminated tomorrow, why do I owe any loyalty to a company that doesn't give loyalty to me? And, why should I form close bonds with a team of co-workers, when we're all likely to scatter to the four winds at any moment?"

An expert in organizational behavior at Cornell University observed, "Leading Millennials requires not only directing them, but also winning them over by pitching your ideas... They don't want you to give them power. They want you to recognize their power...through partnership."[25]

For these reasons, Millennials, Gen-Xers and younger generations respond well to Democratic leadership, but it has to be genuine – not just a superficial pretense of asking for their opinions.

They also respond well to Pacesetting leadership styles, but only if the leader takes the trouble to get their buy-in to a goal or project. That often means selling the idea to your team in terms of the greater good for society and the social-service aspect of a goal.

---

25   Samuel Bacharach, "How to Lead Millennials," *Inc. Magazine,* October 2014. www.inc.com/sam-bacharach/how-to-lead-millennials.html

Leading by gender: how can leaders encourage more women to speak up?

When it comes to working with women, many leaders – especially men -- may need to make a special effort to solicit female input. This certainly includes encouraging more women to speak out and stand up for themselves in a group meeting or in a team environment.

Yes, it is absolutely true that there are lots of self-confident, super-articulate women out there who will speak just as quickly – and just as forcefully – as men. And, when they speak, these women cite just as much logic and research to back up their views.

At the same time, numerous studies show that "on the whole," women tend to be more self-critical, expect to be judged more harshly, and get interrupted or disregarded more than men. Women therefore tend to hold back more. When they do speak up, many women prefer to prepare their remarks in advance so they can bullet-proof them against expected criticism. They may not feel as comfortable as men, shooting from the hip.[26]

Setting meetings with agendas clearly announced in advance is a major service to team members who have these concerns. Another factor that strengthens women is to put more of them into a group. A lone woman on a team of men often feels outnumbered, and remains silent.

But when there are three or four women, or better yet a majority of women, in a group discussion, they feel supported – and therefore, they often feel confident enough to speak out and offer their best input. Award-winning research bears this out.[27]

---

26   Chitra Reddy, "Why Women Don't Speak Up at Work or High-Level Meetings." https://content.wisestep.com/dont-women-speak-work-high-level-meetings/

27   Brittany Karford Rogers, "How to lead Women," BYU Magazine, Spring 2020.

https://magazine.byu.edu/article/when-women-dont-speak/. Also: Tali Mendelberg, Christopher Karpowitz and J. Baxter Oliphant,

"Gender Inequality in Deliberation: Unpacking the Black Box of Interaction." Copyright American Political Science Association.

With these factors in mind, what leadership tools, techniques and styles work best for women?

Again, any style can work depending on the goal, the personalities and the environment involved in a specific situation. Nevertheless, it appears that many women may benefit especially from the Democratic leadership style, especially the kind that makes it a "rule" or expectation that everyone must state their opinion.

Even more interesting is what happens when a group decides it must reach its decisions with <u>unanimous agreement</u> from everyone at the table. This is a natural fit for the Affiliative leadership style. While insisting on consensus can have drawbacks (as discussed earlier), it's sometimes a good exercise because it surfaces issues, ideas, and possibilities that would not otherwise have been brought up.

Leadership for teams that are culturally, racially or ethnically diverse

As most people know who are alive in the 21st century, dealing with a diverse society or a diverse workforce can be a minefield. It's a minefield because we all make so many unconscious assumptions about each other, and because – let's face it – the rules keep changing.

For example, for much of the 20th century, a white middle-class person who meets someone else (of any race) often used a standard opening ice-breaker question: "What do you do?"

In the questioner's mind, this was a neutral question. It did _not_ equate to "How much money do you earn?" Another positive thing about this question was that it showed personal interest. It gave the person who answered a chance to reveal something about themselves, based on the assumption that most people perform work of some kind that they like or find interesting.

Cambridge University Press: https://www.cambridge.org/core/journals/perspectives-on-politics/article/gender-inequality-in-deliberation-unpacking-the-black-box-of-interaction/7C72D50D31CE-C1330B58F0BDA4F9084B

But 20 years ago, a black friend told me, "I wish so many white folks didn't always start a conversation by asking, 'What do you do?' Black folks tend to hear that as, 'How much money do you make?'"

In other words, the effect was *exactly the opposite* of what was intended. My friend suggested whites should ask a different question instead, one that he viewed as more neutral: "Where are you from?"

Still, times change, and recently I noticed a national broadcast interview where a black organization's spokesperson said, "White folks should stop asking black people, 'Where are you from?' It comes off like, 'Do you live in a high-income zip code or a low-income zip code'?"

At this point, the only safe opening question may be, "How are you?" (and I'm not even sure about that). How does a successful leader navigate this ever-shifting minefield of race relations, cultural diversity and ethnic diversity?

There are no easy answers. Diversity training at larger companies has become a standard part of any attempted solution, but at best it's a beginning, not an end. Here are some group icebreakers that have worked for some leaders:

1) *Get the subject out in the open*. Call a meeting to talk about it. Acknowledge that "We have people in this organization from many different backgrounds, races and cultures, and that's a good thing. The better we understand each other, the stronger we are as a team."

   Then encourage people to talk about themselves or tell stories about their families or their culture. (Hint: plant some speakers in advance who agree to speak up; don't spring this on the whole group cold).

2) *Celebrate differences*. One organization held a different "Heritage Day" each month. January 28th was Korean Heritage Day; February 26th was Irish Heritage Day; March 25th was Mexican Heritage Day. On that day, members of the

particular ethnic or cultural group that was being celebrated, brought in party food that represented their background. Also, someone from that ethnic or cultural group made a five-minute presentation based on cultural sharing. That might include performing or playing music from the Old Country, showing "home" clothing styles, or even demonstrating marital arts skills.

3) *Take a cue from the Armed Forces*. The United States Military Leadership Diversity Commission noted in a recent paper that "assimilation" (forcing minorities to conform to the majority's norms) is very different from "inclusion" (which the Commission said *"preserves and leverages individual differences"* in service of group goals and effectiveness).

This is about a mindset first and foremost. But the Commission pointed to successful U.S. Air Force officers who put that mindset into practice in a very down-to-earth way, leading their diverse teams by being "intensely focused on their people, rather than processes or administration."

Specific people-focused practices cited as effective by the Commission included, "Instill a mission-related sense of identity; manage work-group processes; facilitate communication; motivate in accord with needs/goals; provide the tools to do the job; and establish personal and professional credibility."[28]

Again, these three suggestions are basically icebreakers and starting points for what is sure to be a long and continuing journey to great leadership of diverse teams and organizations.

Despite the size and duration of the challenge, a successful leader in today's diverse society commits to taking this journey, and he or she

---

28   Military Leadership Diversity Commission, Issue Paper #29: "Effective Diversity Leadership – Definition and Practices." https://diversity.defense.gov/Portals/51/Documents/Resources/Commission/docs/Issue%20Papers/Paper%2029%20-%20Effective%20Diversity%20Leadership.pdf

makes a start, however small it may be. "The journey of a thousand miles begins with a single step."

This a long and sometimes tough road -- but the rewards can be incredible

As you begin taking your first steps down this trail of "leadership for diversity," be prepared for surprises – some painful, some wonderful. Above all keep in mind three reasons why this journey is crucially important for you as a leader in the 21st century:

Reason #1 -- In America's 10 largest metropolitan areas, 50% of the people are multicultural.[29]

Reason #2 -- Women are purchasers or joint decision-makers in 80% of all major purchases.[30]

Reason #3 -- Millennials became largest living generation in 2016, with annual purchase power of more than $2.5 trillion.[31]

In other words, tomorrow's <u>followers</u> are already here. Tomorrow's Leader is tasked with going out to meet them, recruit them, sell them, and lead them. (And promote them to leadership in their own right).

That leads us to a core question. What is the single *most critical ingredient of leadership* that enables you to embrace the diverse workforce of today and shape its members into effective teams?

Surprisingly, perhaps, the most crucial ingredient for success in this arena is not any strategy, style, or three-point plan. It's a simple yet profound value called TRUST.

Trust is what we'll address in our next chapter -- and it's your next big waystation on the road to becoming Tomorrow's Leader.

---

29   Tariq Khan, Are You Hiring more multicultural (workers), women and millennials? https://www.nxtbook.com/ygsreprints/GAMA/G111479_gama_nov2019/index.php#/p/44
30   Ibid.
31   Ibid.

Trust is the Oil in the Engine: Creating a Culture of Leadership

Teams only follow leaders they trust. Earning trust is the first and most important step in creating a culture of leadership.

Sara Mathew had a giant problem. She had recently joined Dun & Bradstreet, the famous corporation that provides commercial data and ratings for more than 250 million businesses worldwide. A high "D&B" rating of creditworthiness is the gold standard of financial soundness and investor trust.

But what if D&B itself was built on a foundation of shaky numbers?

That disturbing possibility is what Sara uncovered, a year or so after she became the company's Chief Financial Officer in 2001.

Investigating some numbers that didn't quite add up, Sara and her newly installed team of finance geeks gradually realized that D&B had been *using the wrong accounting procedures* for several years, causing the company to significantly overstate its earnings in several areas.

Sara and her team saw no evidence of fraud. The problem appeared to have happened because accounting at this level is so incredibly complex, even world-class executives can make subtle – yet massive -- mistakes at times. This, unfortunately, was one of those times.

Together, D&B's accounting errors and subsequent misreporting of earnings added up to many millions of dollars in overstated revenues, going back several years. At first Sara didn't know just how much damage had been done, but she realized immediately that D&B faced three unappetizing choices.

Choice number one, <u>ignore the problem</u>.

Choice number two, <u>investigate half-heartedly</u> (and then back off if the results were too overwhelming and wait for the market to sniff out the problem by itself).

Choice number three, conduct a fearless investigation, document all the facts no matter how bad they looked, and then <u>come clean</u> with the market and regulators as soon as possible.

The timing for D&B could hardly have been worse. Enron, the giant energy company, had just gone bankrupt because of fraudulent accounting. In fact, Enron was forced to restate its earnings and file the largest bankruptcy in economic history.

Understandably, the market was jittery.

Sara went to D&B's Chairman and CEO, Allen Loren, who had only been with the company a year longer than Sara. Sara explained the problem.

What do you think we should do? said Allen.

Sara made the gutsy call. She said there really was no option: D&B had to go with choice number three, discover all the facts and then report the truth, the whole truth, and nothing but the truth – even if it hurt the company's stock value.

Allen Loren concurred. Six weeks later, on Feb. 5, 2003 (D&B's next quarterly earnings call), the company boldly informed investors and the world that over the past decade it had overstated its earnings to the tune of $150 million. No fraud was found.

Despite Enron poisoning the atmosphere, the market responded as positively to this news as Sara and Allen had hoped. Investors recognized that a new team had come in, found a problem, and courageously stepped up to be transparent and fix the problem with impressive speed.

Amazingly, as a direct result of this approach, D&B's stock value remained rock-steady. Not only did the company maintain full share price, but most crucially, it retained the most priceless asset of all: its reputation for truth, integrity, honesty, and trustworthiness.

There were personal rewards for D&B's transparent performance, as well. By 2007, Sara was made President of the company — and in 2010 she was also elevated to Chairman.

When trust is present, a leader can survive almost any crisis. When trust is missing, failure is just a matter of time

The story of Sara Mathews and D&B's brave restatement of its earnings points to a powerful insight about leadership.

While there is no doubt that successful leadership demands vision, decisiveness, and all the rest, above all it requires followership. That is something that must be earned, and there is only one way for a leader to earn it. Team members must have trust in their leader, period, or else they don't have a leader — they just have someone telling them what to do, whom they may or may not listen to.

When leaders are transparent and share all the relevant facts with their team, insofar as possible, then their followers will walk through walls for them. But when leaders are not transparent, trust is undermined. Team members start cutting corners and hiding information themselves. (After all, they're only emulating the example set by leadership).

Eventually, in an atmosphere where trust is lacking, many team members will start looking for the exit. At that point, it is no longer a question of "if" the organization will fail; it is only a question of "when."

In D&B's case, the "followers" included not only company employees, but also investors, stockbrokers, hedge fund managers, and government regulators – all of whom had the power to make or break D&B's future, depending on whether or not they believed the company was trustworthy.

By acting with integrity, Sara Mathews and Allen Loren earned trust from all of these entities. They also set a powerful example of integrity for the company's workforce of 600 people. There was no doubt in the minds of any employee at Dun & Bradstreet what the company's culture was based on. It was based on truth, honesty and transparency.

They saw that acting with integrity and trustworthiness was valued, indeed expected – and rewarded. As a result, D&B maintained its sterling reputation and those values were upheld by everyone who worked there.

For any organization, team, or leader, there is no stronger foundation than trust.

Trust makes "blind faith" possible, and successful leaders must sometimes ask their followers to give them that faith

I have spent most of my career in highly competitive, financial sales organizations, and I'm proud of it. But one thing I've learned is that in a specialized field like mine, the road to sales success for an individual executive or team member is not always obvious.

Particularly in the beginning of their careers, sales professionals in certain fields must often do many things that don't have an immediate payoff, and may seem pointless. If they trust the leader who urges them to invest time and effort in cultivating long-term relationships with non-buyers who just happen to be well-connected to lots of potential buyers, then three or four years into their career, something great happens. These journeymen sales associates find themselves getting lots of referrals to qualified buyers, who call them and ask to do business. They rapidly begin enjoying the rewards of building a large, lucrative client base.

Sometimes, however, trainees in my industry decide not to put in the time and effort to cultivate these long-term relationships. They refuse to do so because (a) there's no instant gratification in cultivating relationships with people who can't or won't "buy right now"; (b) it's really hard work; and (c) above all, they don't trust the leader who says, "Trust me, doing this will guarantee your success."

When followers don't trust their leaders on this crucial guidance, then something terrible happens by their second, third or fourth year. Their careers stall. Nobody is calling them. There is no organic growth in their client base – which is the only kind that works.

Result: they either have to start over at the beginning and take care of the fundamentals, or drop out of the industry and find another career.

When followers trust a leader even when they can't see immediate justification or results for doing so, I call this "blind faith."

An inspiring example of "blind faith" – the Blue Angels flying 500 mph, 36 inches apart

One of the most dramatic and exciting examples of blind faith that I know is the U.S. Navy's "Blue Angels" high-performance flight demonstration squadron.

The Angels' daily practice regimen begins with a "virtual" or imaginary flight exercise. All of the pilots sit in a room together, closing their eyes and imagining flying their jets while the leader talks them through each maneuver.

As they perform each imaginary twist, turn, dive and loop, the pilots move their hands in the air in the exact same way that they will soon be moving the wings of their aircraft – just a little slower!

Crucially, once these superb pilots are in the air, only the leader can look ahead. Each following aircraft pilot must keep "eyes right" or "eyes left" as appropriate, focusing on the nearest wing of the aircraft beside them. This is the only way to fly 500 miles per hour with planes that are only 18 to 36 inches apart, and maintain perfect formation with flawless safety.

The pilots must trust their leader to be their "eyes forward," and to call out the commands and orders at the right time and place. These Navy aviators are almost literally putting their lives in the squadron leader's hands (and eyes).

That is the power of blind faith when exercised by a leader who has earned the trust of their followers!

5 leadership actions that create trust... and the 5 leadership failures that destroy trust

Since trust is so crucial to successful leadership, how does a great leader go about earning it from his or her followers? There are some basic steps that go 90% of the way toward creating trust. When you think about it, many of these steps may seem obvious, but we tend to underrate their importance.

However, when you add all the steps together, that's when the magic happens. Trust is created -- and leaders can look over their shoulders to find their team is gung-ho behind them, even in tough situations.

To build trust:

1) *Be transparent.*

The Sara Mathews and Allen Loren story at D&B is an outstanding example of the power of transparency. Transparency means sharing the bad news as well as the good. It also means letting your team in on your plans and strategy, as much as you can and to the degree that it will be helpful to your team.

2) *Know what you're talking about. Then, teach it.*

Be knowledgeable about your field, and be ready to share that knowledge whenever a team member asks for help, or when you can see they need some guidance. Giving personal examples from your own experience is highly conducive to building trust in what you say.

3) *Demonstrate in action that you know what you're talking about.*

Teaching and explaining are good, but active demonstrations are priceless reinforcers of any lesson you're trying to teach. I once knew the sales manager for a boiler room, cold-calling operation at TIME/Life Books. His top lesson to his team was this: *"Great books don't sell books. Confidence on the part of the salesperson sells books."*

Whenever sales lagged, the sales crew began blaming lousy leads. The manager would emerge from his office overlooking the bullpen and challenge his team, "Give me the worst lead you've got, and make up the stupidest book title you can think of."

He then proceeded to call whatever phone number he was given and to sell whoever answered the phone a non-existent book called "Hungarian Goulash Cooking," or some equally ridiculous, made-up title. He always closed the sale in about 30 seconds. (TIME/Life never charged any customer for these mythical books, of course.)

The sales team was always delighted and impressed by this active show of irresistible self-confidence and its results. With their trust in the system restored, sales bounced back to their normal levels in minutes. To earn trust, demonstrate your truth in action!

4) *Be trustworthy in small things, to be trustworthy in all things*.

Leaders who cut corners on "unimportant" items, whether it's expenses or paperwork or punching the clock – or anything else – end up squandering their team's trust when they ask for faith and followership on big things, like sacrificing extra hours and weekends to achieve some crucial goal. For a successful leader, there is no such thing as a "small" or insignificant lapse in truthfulness.

5) *Make it personal, and have total personal integrity*.

People don't trust leaders they don't feel they know personally. Your private life may have nothing to do with your work in a formal or legalistic sense, but in terms of the psychology of your followers, there is nothing like self-disclosure to make people feel they can trust you.

I know a woman – we'll call her "Liz" – who was Chief Financial Officer at a manufacturing company. Liz was promoted to temporary CEO when the boss retired suddenly for health reasons. Unlike the retiring CEO, Liz got to know every worker in the plant, learned their names, shook their hands, asked about their families, and treated every one of them with interest and respect. She even brought her parents to the factory to show them the organization that she was leading, and to introduce them to everyone.

The week after Liz became the "temp CEO," the company's union workforce went on strike. Liz was forced to engage in weeks of contentious, exhausting round-the-clock negotiations.

She did not blame the unions; she understood the game. She said: "Union leaders need to be able to go back to their members and say, 'We really beat up management 24 hours a day for weeks and weeks, until they finally broke down and gave us the best possible deal.'"

After two months of arguing and bargaining, it was 4:00 in the morning and both sides were at the bargaining table. This particular negotiating session had been going for 18 hours straight, and there was no end in sight.

"I was so tired I didn't know what I was saying anymore," recalls Liz. "I was just babbling at that point. Suddenly the union boss jumped up said, 'Liz, stop! Stop! We'll sign the contract with the terms you have proposed.'

"I said, WHAT? You will? WHY?

"He said, 'Because of what you just said.'

"I said, 'What did I just say?'

"He said: "Liz, you said – *'Joe, I swear on my mother's life this is the best deal I've got. I really don't know how I can improve on these terms.'* I have met your mother, Liz, and I know how much she means to you. That is how I know you are telling the truth, and this is your absolute, bottom-line best offer. On that basis, we will be delighted to accept this deal.'"

There is <u>nothing</u> like a personal relationship to build and cement trust.

Naturally, the fastest way to destroy trust is to do the reverse of the steps that we just covered. Specifically...

1) *Be secretive. Hoard all the information you can.*

There is a difference between maintaining a confidence, and keeping secrets from your team. If they have the need to know, then they have the right to know – regardless of whether the facts are good or bad.

The truth always comes out sooner or later, but the leader who tries to hide facts that should be shared with the team, needlessly squanders trust. And once squandered, trust is nearly impossible to get back.

2) *Fake it till you make it.*

This philosophy may work for first-timers and neophytes, but by the time you're a leader, you're supposed to be a genuine expert in something.

No, you don't have to know every detail of every job. In fact, it's much better if you don't. Let the engineers be the engineers, and let the marketing people be the marketing people – but you be the expert on strategy and tactics, and be able to teach what you know in clear, simple language to each member of your team.

3) *Just give orders. Never perform a task someone else can do.*

Want to lose trust in a hurry? It's easy. Just behave like the Wizard of Oz, barking orders from behind a smokescreen and never doing anything yourself. Never put your shoulder to the wheel; never work side by side with your team.

If you want to throw away trust with both hands, stay in your ivory tower or hide in your office, and just send out orders. Or, call people into meetings and tell them what to do, without ever personally joining forces with them on a single project.

4) *Cheat on the small stuff.*

Trust is eroded when leaders cut corners in small things, whether it's padding their expense accounts or pilfering supplies from the office stockroom for personal use. People always find out. Understandably, many team members figure, "If my leader will cheat on something small, he'll cheat on something big."

About two minutes later, they suddenly think: "Hey! Maybe he's cheating ME in some way!"

5) *Remain aloof and impersonal.*

Some leaders have the mistaken notion that effective leadership requires them to maintain a cool, correct distance from the riffraff and the mere human beings who are their followers. This is the "leadership mystique" school of thinking, and it's fatal to earning trust.

Such aloof leaders may think they're being regal and magisterial with their lofty pose. But they are usually perceived by their team members as snobby and standoffish. Their behavior prompts team members to ask, "If I don't know them, how can I trust them?"

Building a culture of leadership is about the intangible vibe that makes everyone feel great about your organization

When a leader works at being trustworthy, and earns real trust from team members, allies, clients and customers, then that leader has gone at least 50% of the way toward creating a healthy culture of leadership.

The other 50% is about atmospherics and policies. Most of the policy questions are basic good management, so we need not discuss them here. But establishing the right atmospherics is another crucial – yet often underrated – factor in exercising successful leadership.

Perhaps the most vivid way to convey the power of organizational "culture" is with a few concrete examples. I once walked into an office where management had just replaced the receptionist with a robot. I am not kidding. The robot was mostly an interactive TV screen, which the visitor was supposed to talk to, ask questions of, and get information from.

Management thought it was great. They loved the money saved on the receptionist's salary and benefits. They also thought the hi-tech approach made their company seem cool and cutting-edge.

A few techno-nerds loved it, too. Unfortunately, this company's customers were not techno-nerds. They were ordinary people – and most of them hated the Robot Receptionist. Some walked in, took one look, and waked out, never to return. That was a culture of leadership, all right – it led customers straight to their competitors!

In contrast, we have all visited offices and organizations that have a great vibe. You walk in and the décor is warm and tasteful, well-lit, with plenty of space, clean comfortable furniture, and carpets and window treatments that look reasonably new or super well-maintained.

Above all, there is someone who greets you with a genuine smile and who is eager and qualified to help you – answering your questions, taking your payment, consulting on who you should talk to, directing you to company brochures if appropriate, and engaging in personal chit-chat to help you feel more relaxed if you're there for some nerve-wracking purpose – such as a first-ever financial planning session, or perhaps a medical consultation about a heart condition.

This same office has workers who are obviously happy to be there, appropriately dressed for that industry or trade, friendly and approachable, and who give an immediate impression of professionalism and success.

That is a place where people want to work. It's also a place where customers and clients want to do business. You have a good experience there from the first moment you arrive, and you probably come back.

Every culture of leadership begins with – you guessed it -- the leader

Ralph Waldo Emerson, America's great 19th century philosopher, once said, "An organization is the lengthened shadow of one man." (Today, of course, Emerson would say: "An organization is the lengthened shadow of one person").

Leaders create culture without even trying. If the leader is eager, upbeat, friendly and enthusiastic, and above all knowledgeable and professional, they set the tone for the team, who will naturally emulate these qualities.

If the leader is grumpy, sour, depressed, short-tempered and uncommunicative, then the team will be too. No matter how great the art on the walls, no matter how much the receptionist plasters a phony smile on his or her face, the cultural vibe of that organization will be negative. Nobody will want to be there, or to work with that organization, for reasons that are all too obvious.

Here's another example: I once knew a company of bright, cheerful, hardworking people who were led by a couple of dysfunctional workaholics. Leaders and team members alike prided themselves on being "crazy busy" all the time. *"How are we? Oh, we're just crazy busy!"* the company leaders loved to say. Soon the staff was saying it too.

In practice, however, this meant the entire team spent every minute scrambling, putting out fires, and responding to emergencies that were created solely through lack of planning and foresight, and lack of sensible, orderly systems for predictable, repeated work requirements.

"Crazy busy" meant a team that -- precisely because its members were hardworking and dedicated -- was constantly on the edge of nervous exhaustion. Temper blow-ups and tears were not unheard of in this organization. Nerves were frayed at the best of times, and screw-ups happened constantly, because team members were too distracted, too busy, or too tired to catch problems that should have been easy to spot, fix or prevent.

At the same time that I worked with this "crazy busy" organization, I also worked with another organization that was just the opposite in terms of its style and culture. These people were top professionals, too -- but they had systems and procedures in place that were time-tested and took human nature into account.

These guys thought "crazy busy" was strictly for amateurs. They took quiet pride in a "no hurry, no worry" vibe of calm competence. Without any muss or fuss, they got every single job done on time -- usually well ahead of time, in fact. Nobody ever caught them staying late, working weekends, or having nervous breakdowns – because they didn't.

This organization knew that at the highest level, the ultimate professionalism looks effortless, even if such "effortlessness" is a bit of an illusion, created by supreme competence and superb managerial acumen that runs the show behind the scenes.

A healthy culture of leadership is also big on teambuilding, and this too begins with the leader. If he or she participates and shows enthusiasm for teambuilding activities, the followers will too.

Again, this involves personal sharing and getting to know people beyond their work roles. This explains why countless successful organizations across this country have happy hours, wacky lunchtime parties, bowling nights, pancake breakfasts, group walks, monthly Team Olympics in the office (or outdoors), and other ice-breaker activities as part of their regular social calendar.

What have such activities got to do with work? Nothing, if considered from a narrow, green-eyeshade perspective.

Everything, if considered from a trust-building, human psychology point of view.

How to tell that you have created a successful culture of leadership

GE's legendary Chairman Jack Welch had a good test for whether or not his company or its divisions or branches were fostering a successful and healthy culture of leadership. He measured GE's internal culture by the sales volume of GE t-shirts and baseball caps to employees.

When team members were buying a lot of these items, Welch knew they were proud of their company, enjoyed working there, and felt good about the place. When sales were low, he knew the opposite was true, or at least in danger of becoming true.

Today's equivalent might be how often team members put something work-related on their social media accounts. Few things say *"I'm proud of my work and committed to our mission"* like a tweet or a Facebook post.

Referrals from current and past employees and customers are also a classic measurement of a healthy culture of leadership. Another traditional yardstick is, do people show up early and stay late? (But be careful, because this gauge can seriously underrate the enthusiasm and commitment of team members who are phenomenally efficient and productive, accomplishing far more work and creating far more value, in far less time than the ordinary team member).

Another good measure of the health of a culture of leadership is to look around to see how much effort team members devote to mentoring and helping each other. If such activity occurs frequently in your organization, then you probably have a superb culture of leadership.

Most of all, when competitors start copying your style, your management philosophy. and your organizational structure, then you can probably give yourself five gold stars for leadership culture.

An outstanding case study in creating a culture of leadership: the astonishing turnaround of the *USS Benfold*

In June of 1997, U.S. Navy Captain D. Michael Abrashoff took command of the *USS Benfold,* a 500-foot-long, 8,000-ton destroyer armed with 18 guns, a guided missile launch system, and a crew of 310 sailors

— including 33 commissioned officers, 38 chief petty officers and 210 enlisted personnel.

It was a proud moment for Captain Abrashoff, until he witnessed the crew's jeering disrespect for their departing commander. Then Abrashoff learned that the *Benfold* ranked near the bottom of the Pacific Fleet in terms of performance.

Subsequent investigations told Captain Abrashoff that the ship's crew had been subjected to a terrible culture of tyranny and petty bullying from his predecessor, rather than true leadership.

Abrashoff dug deep and turned the situation around with an enlightened attitude of "servant leadership." He began by really listening to the concerns of his crew. He followed up by working his tail off to get his team the things they wanted and needed. Like better educational opportunities. Like less time spent on pointless activities such as rust-scraping, painting and repainting the same nuts and bolts — replacing them with rustproof stainless steel instead. And, like encouraging everyone to take pride in excellence, viewing the ship as an extension of themselves.

The good captain told his crew two things over and over. First, "It's your ship" — meaning you guys ultimately control the destiny of the *Benfold,* not me. Second, he urged crewmembers to adopt the goal of making their vessel "the best damn ship in the Navy."

Eventually, the crew heard these slogans so often, they started to believe them. And then, they started to act upon them.

Working together, the captain and crew achieved a remarkable transformation in record time. A rebellious, resentful, under-performing team turned the *Benfold* into an award-winning vessel one year later, taking top Navy honors in gunnery. (They also saved significant time and money by switching to those stainless-steel nuts and bolts, which every U.S. Navy ship now uses.)

Captain Abrashoff explained his culture of leadership this way:

"My ship's job was war; your company's purpose is profit. But we will achieve neither by ordering people to perform as we wish. Even if doing so produces short-term benefits, the consequences can prove devastating.

"My experience has shown that helping people realize their full potential can lead to attaining goals that would be impossible to reach under [a leadership culture of] command-and-control."[32]

The story of the *USS Benfold* is an amazing lesson in how a wise leader can completely change an organization's culture, without changing any of its people (i.e., no hiring and firing).

Captain Abrashoff did everything right. He had a vision and shared it, passionately and repeatedly. It was a simple, easy-to-understand vision. It touched everything about the ship and its crew – how it looked, felt, acted, and regarded itself.

He fostered teamwork and mutual support. He provided individual attention and care, not barking commands but sitting down with each crew member and getting to know them personally – i.e., more than 300 men and women.

The result was that the *Benfold's* crew did the single greatest thing that culture is supposed to do: internalize the vision in the hearts of each member of the organization, so that they were personally committed to upholding a common set of values and working cooperatively for a common goal.

---

32   Captain D. Michael Abrashoff, "It's Your Ship: Management Techniques from the Best Damn Ship in the Navy." Warner Books, 2002.

When Captain Abrashoff's tour as commander of the ship ended, he skipped the traditional ceremony with flags and a Navy band and dress whites and lots of saluting and flowery speeches.

Instead, he used the savings from those stainless-steel nuts and bolts to fly in 300+ lobster dinners for his entire crew. At his going-away dinner, he stood up and gave what some observers claim is the shortest farewell address in the history of the United States Navy. It was just 5 words: "You know how I feel."

Captain Abrashoff and the proud crew of the *USS Benfold* have a mighty lesson to teach all of us. If leadership is about earning trust, they proved that it's a two-way street – and that anyone can spot a healthy, successful culture of leadership a mile away, when it begins with genuine respect and pride in yourself and your organization.

Looking forward: the job of the leader includes marking a clear, simple path to the ultimate destination

On your journey of leadership, you can travel by Blue Angels jet, by Navy destroyer, by spending 24/7 at the bargaining table, or on foot. You can work on Wall Street or run a mom and pop hardware store. You can be a family leader or a community leader.

What matters for leadership is not where we work or how we travel.

- What matters is realizing the crucial importance of building relationships with our team members that are solidly based on trust.

- What matters is that we understand the inestimable value of building a culture of leadership that instills a shared vision in each and every team member.

With these strengths in your toolkit, you are ready to travel down the next challenging stretch of road with your team. The upcoming phase of your journey is about marking out a clear path with clear, simple steps to the goal -- no matter how difficult, complex or super-sophisticated your ultimate goal may be.

The focus of our next chapter is mapmaking, with an emphasis on "the beauty of simplicity and the agony of complexity." Buckle up, because it's going to be a fast ride!

CHAPTER 11

Successful leaders embrace "the beauty of simplicity" and avoid "the agony of complexity"

Complexity is often needlessly confusing. Successful leaders and their teams seek to "become brilliant at the basics."

In this chapter we're going to discover why simpler is better — and why an important task for any successful leader is to simplify things.

By the way, this holds true for team members at every level, whether they are leaders, engineers, marketers, financial wizards, management, production workers, HR people, you name it.

It even applies to salespeople in golf club specialty stores, as I learned one day when I attempted to buy a new set of clubs. I ran into a salesman who made the whole process so needlessly complicated that it became baffling for me, and then frustrating.

Viewed in retrospect, this incident is amusing — and instructive, because it teaches an important lesson about "the beauty of simplicity and the agony of complexity."

How a needlessly complex sales presentation stopped me from buying a set of golf clubs

I must have been the world's easiest customer on that day when I walked into the Callaway golf club specialty store. I was not window-shopping. I had done my research. I knew exactly what I wanted. I was ready to order and pay.

I'm a tall guy, six foot three, so I told the salesman that I would need my clubs measured and fitted. I said I thought I might need an inch added to each club but I wasn't sure.

"Great," he said. He gave me a standard-sized driver and said, "Come to the back of the store, where you can swing the club." I followed him there and he said, "Okay, swing it. Let me take a look."

I swung the club for a little bit. The sales guy watched and said, "You're right, you need an inch added onto each club."

I said, "Okay, sounds good. Let's do it."

He said, "But you know, keep swinging it for a little bit."

I kept swinging and swinging the club. Finally the salesman said, "Well, you probably need an inch added to the shorter irons, but the longer irons are probably fine as they are."

I said, "Oh, okay."

And he said, "But keep swinging." And I swung the club a little bit more.

Then he said, "You know what, you probably might not even need any change. You might be able to be fine with them as they are."

And I'm like, what?

Now he took the club and started swinging it himself. Frankly, by this point he was confusing the heck out of me. I'm not an expert on fitting golf clubs. I didn't know precisely what the best fit would be or what I needed. I was looking to this supposed expert for the help -- and now he couldn't even make up its own mind!

I ended up leaving that store. I went to right down the street to their competitor. I walked in and said, "I know what clubs I want, and I need them fitted."

The salesman said, "Great." He had me swing the club while he observed. He said, "You need an inch on every club. Yep, I'm sure."

I said, "Okay, sold."

And I got my clubs. They worked fine on the golf course, by the way.

Why so many very smart leaders fail to embrace simplicity

You can be sure that some variation on this story plays out in every kind of organization in the world, hundreds if not thousands of times a day.

Perhaps a financial advisor over-explains the market to a potential client, trying to show off all the depth and detail that they know. They end up talking the client out of the move they're recommending. They might even talk a prospect out of becoming a customer in the first place.

Or, a car sales pro ruins a presentation by talking too much and overselling. Or a doctor scares off a patient by drowning them in medical detail when all the patient needs is a simple, clear, one-pointed diagnosis.

Why do so many leaders and professionals fall into the trap of need-less complexity, and thereby set up counterproductive results for themselves and their team? There are several reasons:

- Some leaders are too confused in their own thinking to achieve simplicity. They can't make things clear to their followers (or to sales prospects), because they don't have it clear in their own minds.

- Some leaders are intellectual snobs. They assume everyone else "should" know what they know. They insist on making others think on their level, even if team members are not qualified to do so – and even if potential clients have <u>no interest</u> in doing so.

- And, some leaders are allergic to simplicity because they're insecure. They have an intellectual bias that "Simple is dumb," and they're afraid that if they make things simple, they will be judged as dumb.

The deadly prejudice against simplicity

For all of these reasons, many leaders in business, government, science, culture and other fields have a strong prejudice *against* simplicity. Some brilliant and highly successful leaders have admitted to me that they are afraid that if their goals or messages sound "too simple," their team members or their audiences will not be impressed.

This may sound strange, but many leaders are desperate to impress others at all costs – yes, even at the cost of clarity, understanding and effectiveness within their own organizations.

These leaders fear that if they don't attempt to dazzle everyone with complex theories, plans and language, then others will assume they are simple-minded, unsophisticated people. So they actively avoid simplicity.

This prejudice against simplicity is a common one, but it's a mental habit that successful leaders either don't have -- or learn to break in a hurry.

> *The truth is, "simple" does not mean "unsophisticated."*

Quite the opposite: at the highest level of thinking and planning, simplicity is the result of deep insight and hard work.

Some of the smartest people on the planet have said so, and some of the most advanced technology companies in the world have strongly embraced this philosophy. Let me share three outstanding examples:

- *Steve Jobs and Apple:*

   An Apple iPhone is very simple to use, considering the number and flexibility of its functions and apps. But achieving that (relative) level of intuitive simplicity required tremendous sophistication in design, engineering, marketing and customer psychology.

It was Steve Jobs himself who said: "One of my mantras [has always been] focus and simplicity. Simple can be harder than complex. You have to work hard to get your thinking clean to make it simple. But it's worth it in the end, because once you get there, you can move mountains."[33]

- *Albert Einstein and the Theory of Relativity:*

Einstein's world-famous equation for the Theory of Relativity ($E = MC^2$) is about as simple as it gets. Yet this seemingly simple equation captures one of the most subtle, profound and sophisticated insights in all of human history.

Not only that, but Einstein was perfectly willing to simplify the concept even more, in a humorous way, when non-physicists asked him to explain his famous theory in layman's terms. "When you're talking to a pretty girl, an hour seems like a minute," said Einstein. "But if you're sitting on a hot stove, a minute feels like an hour. That's relativity!"

- *McDonnell Douglas and a single ball bearing:*

For many years, one of the world's leading aviation manufacturers ran the identical, unchanging full-page advertisement every week in industry trade magazines. Their ad showed a gleaming black ball bearing on a deep-blue background. At the bottom of the page was a seven-word message: "In technology, simplicity is the ultimate sophistication." Finally, the ad gave the name of the aircraft company.

That was it! The advertisement itself was an outstanding example of the power of the philosophy that it advocated. (By the way, the line "simplicity is the ultimate sophistication" is

---

33   Gordon Tredgold, "Simplicity Is the Key to Success," *Forbes,* Sept. 19, 2016.

often attributed to Leonardo da Vinci, but there is no proof that da Vinci actually said it or wrote it).

When it comes to simplicity, clear thinking is half the battle. The other half is clear communication

There is one more critical reason why so many leaders -- even those who are perfectly secure and not trying to impress anyone -- fall into the trap of needless complexity.

Most people _underestimate_ the difficulty of achieving clear communication, and they _overestimate_ both their own ability to explain an idea, as well as their listeners' ability to follow that idea.

As the witty Irish playwright George Bernard Shaw liked to say, "The single biggest problem in communication is the illusion that it has taken place."

You can greatly increase the odds that your team will understand your message and carry it out more effectively, if you can translate your vision into a _simple_ plan with _simple_ steps. That allows everyone to understand it, remember it and follow it.

Successful leaders know that simplicity is a virtue, even a necessity, _especially_ when your plan is intended to achieve a complex goal that requires a thousand steps, or a million steps, to carry out.

We might even say that the more complex and sophisticated the goal, the simpler its expression (and the plan for achieving it) should be.

Here is a list of proven strategies that you can employ to make sure simplicity is one of the most powerful tools in your leadership toolbox.

10 "simple" steps that will help you leverage simplicity as an advanced leadership tactic

The following 10 steps to achieve simplicity as a leadership technique may sound like common sense, but they are a lifetime's work. Each step is something that every successful leader tries to continually improve at executing. Successful leaders know the payoff for simplicity is superior motivation for their team, unmatched effectiveness for their organization, and achieving goals faster and more completely.

Smart leaders continue working at simplicity all through their careers because -- as you'll see -- even great leaders can flub one or more of these 10 steps. Simplicity is hard!

Step 1: Clearly define the problem

Begin by <u>clearly defining the problem you're trying to solve</u>. Get the definition on one page or less. Half a page is even better, a paragraph is great, and fully defining the problem that you're trying to solve in a single sentence is genius.

This principle of "define the problem in one page or less" may sound like a superficial gimmick. I assure you it's not; this is a serious management tool that has been embraced and promoted by some of the most successful leaders in many fields.

An outstanding example is Ralph Bahna, the business wizard who single-handedly invented Business Class air travel and in the process, turned around one of the major U.S. airlines from failing to dominating the market for several years. Then Ralph reinvented cruise ships as "floating resorts" and saved that entire industry with a strategy they still use today.

In his later years, Ralph spent much of his time teaching business wisdom at top colleges around the U.S. This "one-page problem definition" advice was at the top of his list.

"The biggest problem that I see with many business leaders, and particularly with startups," said Ralph, "is that they don't have a clear idea of the problem they are trying to solve. If you ask them that question, they spend 10 minutes talking in circles. At the end of that time, you still don't know what they're trying to accomplish.

How can they possibly accomplish it, if they can't even explain their goal or figure out what it is?"

Step 2: Create a plan of actionthat actually addresses the problem

Once you understand the problem you're trying to solve, come up with a plan to solve it — meaning, a plan that directly addresses that problem.

Your proposed solution should not be about falling in love with technology for technology's sake. Your solution should not be about keeping your team members spinning their wheels with lots of motion that makes them look busy, but doesn't add to measurably productive outcomes.

Instead, your proposed solution, and the plan to achieve that solution, should be about actually addressing the problem in the most clear, direct, simple and effective way you and your team can think of.

Step 3: Focus on a single overarching goal

As your plan starts coming into focus, select one overarching goal. Make this your key objective, your ultimate destination. It can be supported by many sub-goals or preliminary steps, but there should be just ONE objective that is the most important, and you should be crystal-clear on what that goal is, and why it's the key to the entire operation.

The story of the *USS Benfold* in the last chapter offered a superb example of this principle in action. The captain's overarching goal was powerful, clear, exciting, and easy to remember and repeat: "Let's make the *Benfold* the best damn ship in the Navy!"

That simplicity of focus, concept and language was a big part of what made the captain's core objective so incredibly motivating for his crew. Naturally, the *Benfold* required a thousand tiny steps to make that goal a reality – but having the goal clearly in everyone's mind, came first.

Step 4: Express your core objective in simple, super-clear terms

It is extremely important for a successful leader to be able to express your overarching goal in <u>unmistakably clear language</u>. In practice, this means learning to use simple, short words and sentences. It also means bear-hugging brevity.

It's no coincidence that most of the great advertising slogans are seven words or less. For example, think of Microsoft's "Where do you want to go today?" and Nike's "Just Do It."

It's also no coincidence that many of the world's top business leaders spend hours and hours honing their "elevator pitch" – a one-minute encapsulation of their key message, which they can give in the time it takes to make a short elevator ride.

Clear communication is a matter of make-or-break importance for a leader. If you want your team to work together effectively, then each member will need a clear, simple understanding of:

a) His or her role in the larger operation;

b) How their work effort contributes to the work being done by other members or people in other divisions; and

c) How their work supports the overall objective.

If you can't explain the overarching objective in clear, simple terms, then you're making it difficult for your team to get a clear picture of how they fit in and how they can maximize their own effectiveness.

Step 5: Lay out a series of intermediate steps to the goal - and keep them simple, too

Support your overarching goal with <u>a series of simple, logical sub-goals or progressive steps</u>. If possible, keep these steps to 10 or less. Here again, less is more. Five steps are better than 10. Two or three steps is best of all.

Selecting the 10 (or fewer) subordinate steps to reach the ultimate destination is an exacting exercise in itself. It requires rigorously clear thinking and a logical understanding of priorities and hierarchies.

For example, "We must first do A before we can move on to step B." Or "While Team A is working on Objective A, Team B will parallel-track their pursuit of Objective B. Then they'll both hand it off to Team C."

Breaking down the journey into simple steps to the ultimate destination is where many plans – even those with a clear, compelling, core objective – often succeed or fail.

In World War II, when the British general Bernard Montgomery dreamed up Operation Market Garden, he had a big, audacious goal clearly in mind, and a big, audacious plan to support it. "Monty" decided to send 35,000 Allied paratroopers into Nazi-occupied Holland, seize all the key bridges, cross the Rhine River into Germany, and defeat the German Army to win the war in Europe by Christmas of 1944.

Unfortunately, the steps to carry out this ultra-ambitious plan were too complex, too dependent on good luck and good weather, and there were far too many "single points of failure" that could bring down the whole house of cards – and did. As one of Monty's subordinates famously said in explaining this fiasco afterwards, "We tried to go a bridge too far."

Step 6: Delegate! (as much as possible)

If sub-sub-steps are needed to carry out your plan and achieve your goal (and they usually are), don't drown people in that level of detail on your first at-bat. Save the depth and details for follow-up meetings.

Often, if you have a competent, well-motivated team, they can figure out the details on their own. A great team can be relied upon to show the initiative to act on those additional needed steps.

Step 7: Communicate like crazy

Explain the major goal and the supporting steps to your team, and continue to reinforce your message by <u>repeating it</u>.

Repetition shows that you mean what you say, that you are truly and deeply committed to the plan, and that you think it's important. It also helps people *understand and remember* the plan. For these reasons, you cannot repeat your basic message too much.

In most cases, you will discover that around the time that you're becoming sick of hearing yourself say the same thing over and over again, that is just when your message is finally starting to really sink in and become part of your team's DNA.

When you hear team members starting to repeat the goal and the plan in largely the same language that you originally used, then you will know that you have achieved actual communication. If this does not take place, then you may have created uncertainty or even confusion.

A good test: have a few one-on-one conversations with different members of your team. Ask them to explain the goal and the plan back to you, as they understand it. If they all say pretty much the same thing, using at least one or two of your key terms or phrases, then you have probably succeeded in communicating a strong, clear, simple vision. If they all give wildly different versions of the story, then you probably need to refocus and reframe your message.

Step 8: State the obvious

When explaining the goal and the plan, don't be afraid of being "too obvious" or "too simple." Remember, people who are steeped in a certain field or culture – especially leaders -- tend to take for granted that everyone else knows what they know, or they unconsciously assume that everyone else has acquired the same instincts they have.

In most cases, this is not true. What seems "obvious" to you may come as a blinding revelation to many others. Don't hesitate to explain the basics. If you're talking to a mixed group with some experts who know the basics, and some journeymen or beginners who don't, then just admit what you're doing: "I realize many of you already know this, but for those of you who may not be familiar with the XYZ Rule, let me explain briefly..."

At the same time, keep in mind that explaining the basics and stating the obvious, is very different from drowning people in detail and teaching a graduate-level seminar to a classroom full of freshmen and sophomores.

Step 9: Clean up your org chart and practice "meeting discipline"

Redundancy is good in communication, but it's potentially fatal in an organization. Eliminate redundancy in your organization and the plan.

It's often confusing and counterproductive to have two team members, or two departments, with heavily overlapping goals and responsibilities. This redundancy leads to turf fights, or conversely it leads to passing the buck. Either way, it creates confusion and working at cross-purposes among the staff. This is a prime example of complexity you don't need.

As for a simple approach to meetings, there is a reason why most people don't love meetings, and why meetings have a reputation as timewasters. Too often, that is exactly what they are.

<u>Keep meetings short and to the point</u>. There is no rule carved in stone that every meeting must be an hour, or even 15 minutes. If you can get the job done in five or 10 minutes, then after that just wrap it up, thank everyone for their attention, and end the meeting.

This not only saves time; it also prevents boredom and energizes your team. As a corollary, only hold meetings when you truly need them. If there is nothing that needs to be discussed this week, cancel the weekly meeting, or send out a memo instead of gathering everyone together.

Voilà! If you have five team members and you cancel a one-hour meeting, then you've just created five hours of extra productivity for your team.

Step 10: Be brilliant at the basics

The executive who personally taught me the most about leadership was Larry Post. He was instrumental in my career and in the careers of hundreds of leaders at Ameriprise. One day at a conference with 500 or so leaders, the president of the company asked anyone who had been developed by Larry over the years to stand up. Over half the room rose to their feet! Larry developed and populated the country with an army of talented leaders, truly an amazing accomplishment.

Simplicity was definitely one of Larry's strongest talents. He frequently urged all of his up-and-coming leaders and hardworking team members to "become brilliant at the basics," by which he meant that we should focus like a laser on core competencies and not get distracted by complex theories, fancy extras, or overly subtle nuances.

As the great old-time football coaches used to say, it's always impressive when your quarterback throws the long bomb and makes the spectacular play. But most games are won in "a cloud of dust and a bucket of blood." In other words, a winning team relies chiefly on its hulking linemen and offensive backs to relentlessly move the ball forward -- a yard at a time, a step at a time, even an inch at a time -- toward the goalpost.

Ask yourself this question: would you like being a passenger in a plane whose pilot knows who to perform complex aerobatics, but who forgets to check the fuel tank? Or would you prefer to be a passenger in a plane whose pilot consistently keeps his eye on the two or three most important indicators and guides the aircraft accordingly?

Pilots who crash due to human error often allow themselves to get distracted by second- and third-tier dials and gauges. As a result, they fail to focus on the two or three indicators that count the most. Or as FAA investigators sometimes say: "He forgot to fly the plane."

The beauty of simplicity

The 10 steps outlined above provide just a few examples that illustrate "the beauty of simplicity" (like Steve Jobs and the iPhone) and "the agony of complexity" (think General Montgomery and "a bridge too far"). You can probably add many more examples of each from your own life and experience.

E. F. Schumacher, the economist and information systems expert who wrote the highly influential book "Small Is Beautiful," once said:

> *"Any intelligent fool can make things bigger, more complex, and more violent.*
>
> *It takes a touch of genius —*
> *and a lot of courage -- to move*
> *in the opposite direction."*

At this point, you're ready to tackle the final step in this book's journey to leadership. The greatest challenge faced by every successful leader, especially in today's world, is the relentless need to cope with changing times, technology and conditions – especially when a crisis erupts.

Our next chapter will focus on making your leadership nimble, flexible, adaptable, forward-thinking – and as crisis-proof as possible!

CHAPTER 12

How successful leaders meet changing times (and cope with a crisis)

Change isn't always welcome or fun. But there are proven ways that leaders can navigate change more easily and successfully.

The average person living in the 16th century – the era of Shakespeare and Queen Elizabeth I – had to absorb less information in their entire lifetime than appears today on the front page of a single edition of the *New York Times*.

This fact got a lot of attention when it appeared in a 1970 book called *Future Shock*, a huge bestseller by business reporter Alvin Toffler.

Toffler was one of the first to point out that people in modern society have to absorb so much change, so fast, and so continually, that the whole world is on the verge of having a permanent nervous breakdown.

Even more impressive, Toffler had this insight decades before the Internet, social media, mobile phones, push notifications, texting, tweeting, Zoom meetings, the end of the Cold War, the rise of China, the advent of genetic engineering and cloning, and all the other revolutionary changes that have flown past and that continue to create earthquakes across global society, every single day.

Today it's a cliché to say that change is a constant factor in our lives. But although everyone acknowledges this fact, most of us are still not great at dealing with it.

Well, that's what leaders are for.

Helping people and organizations cope with change and come through crises, is a huge part of successful leadership.

To get a clear picture of how this works in action, let's look at a super-positive example: Mary Barra, the first woman CEO of a "Big 3" automobile manufacturer.

General Motors CEO Mary Barra sets the standard for coping with changing times – and meeting a crisis head-on

One of the most remarkable stories in the history of American business has got to be the career of Mary Barra, who has been CEO of General Motors since 2014. When Mary stepped up to that role, she became the first woman in history to run one of the world's top three automobile manufacturing companies.

As everyone knows, GM is a giant company founded way back in 1908. In their 396 facilities worldwide, they make 7.7 million vehicles per year, generating annual revenues of $137 billion.

Mary started at GM when she was 18 years old, working part-time to pay for her college education at the GM Institute, now Kettering University. She began by inspecting hoods and fender panels. Over the next 24 years she rose through the ranks in a series of increasingly responsible posts.

She became CEO at a time when GM was not only facing a drastically changing global auto market, but the company was also deep in a crisis.

The industry-rocking change can be summed up as "Tesla and electric vehicles."

The crisis was a faulty GM ignition switch that killed more than a dozen people, leading to the recalls of more than 30 million vehicles. Mary and other GM executives were hauled in front of a U.S. Senate committee in Washington, DC, where lawmakers criticized the company in the most scathing possible terms on live TV.

How did Mary respond to all this? She did not run away from change, deny that electric cars were a serious product, or duck responsibility for the company's self-created crisis. Instead, here's what she did.

1) *To cope with challenging times and new market demands, she embraced change as aggressively as possible.*

   Mary recognized that electric cars were here to stay, and quite possibly could represent the future of the entire car industry. Rather than playing ostrich or talking down Tesla, she got behind GM's own electric vehicle, the Chevrolet Bolt EV, which featured a longer-lasting battery than Tesla's Model 3.

   The Bolt EV rapidly became the bestselling car in its market segment (American non-luxury electric vehicles). In 2016, GM's revenue skyrocketed by 9 percent in a single year, reflecting their largest sales growth in years. They beat Tesla, proving that a gigantic, century-old company could be even more nimble, innovative and disruptive than the most famous, most hyped hi-tech company of the 21st century.

2) *To cope with the safety crisis, Mary embraced transparency and took responsibility.*

   Mary began by ordering a massive internal investigation. What had led to the safety problem with the faulty ignitions in the first place? Who in the company had known about it? Why weren't their warnings heeded?

   She transformed the GM corporate culture so that assembly line workers (like she used to be) could speak up about

> potential problems, and middle management would listen. She also created a victims compensation fund with no limits on payments. Finally, she created a new role for a GM executive who would focus on safety issues companywide.

All of this turned GM around. From 2017 to mid-2018, the company's stock achieved a remarkable 25 percent increase in value.

There are many valuable lessons to learn from Mary's crisis leadership and her leadership in changing, challenging times – and the first lesson is, what is the ultimate job of a leader?

A good answer is that <u>leaders are here to help their organizations do just that: cope with change and overcome crises!</u> And, leaders are here to find the best way across rough terrain to a successful, healthy future.

In changing times, people look to their leaders for guidance

All over the world, 92% of workers say it's vitally important for leaders to respond to challenging times and crises.[34] This means changing times offer a heightened leadership opportunity. When people are living through a tsunami of change, or when their institutions or lives are rocked by a crisis, they are more eager than ever for guidance, and more willing to follow the path set out for them by a strong, visionary leader.

You may be thinking: *Yes, I know that's true because I've seen it. But why? What are the specific reasons why leadership becomes even more important in a crisis than in ordinary times?*

There are many reasons. In a fluid or chaotic situation, such as today's economy where people are changing jobs more often and the corporate norms are shifting from a well-defined career ladder to a "find

---

34 Caroline Castrillon, "How to Cope with Change in the Workplace," *Forbes*, Feb. 26, 2020. *www.forbes. com/sites/carolinecastrillon/2020/02/26/how-to-cope-with-change-in-the-workplace/#68a34498d207*

your own path, set your own hours" culture, human nature remains a constant. We all remember looking to our parents for guidance in new or scary situations, and in tough times for an organization, people fall back on that psychological model. In a family environment, that can mean mom and dad, but in a work environment it means looking to our leaders.

Another reason why people look to leaders for more guidance in changing times is that leaders are supposed to know more and be ready to leverage that knowledge on behalf of the group. Even if they don't actually know more about the specific issue at hand (which could be brand-new and totally unprecedented), leaders are tasked with being the right person to learn the new landscape and wisely evaluate the terrain, scoping out potential dangers and opportunities.

In fact, according to the *Harvard Business Review*, we can sum it up by saying simply: "Leadership…is about coping with change."[35]

Finally, in challenging circumstances, people look to leaders for emotional cues, emotional support and psychological reassurance. If the leader seems upbeat and optimistic in the face of a challenge, it gives followers encouragement to feel likewise. This points to another crucial aspect of successful leadership in changing or difficult times: coping with stress.

Change also causes stress, so pay attention to the emotional toll. Provide reassurance and inspiration

When a challenging situation arises, leaders aren't just managing organizations or coming up with smart policies. They also realize that part of their job is managing the emotions of their colleagues, team members, customers, clients and allies.

---

35   John P. Kotter, "What Leaders Really Do," *Harvard Business Review*, Dec. 2001 issue. *https://hbr. org/2001/12/what-leaders-really-do*

This is a huge task all by itself, and an extremely important one. Whether you are a leader or a follower, a participant or even just an onlooker, change is, by definition, stressful.

The definition of stress in a work environment is "lots of responsibility, no authority."

According to a 2017 survey by the Harris polling organization, conducted on behalf of the American Psychological Association, "Workers experiencing recent or current change were more than twice as likely to report chronic work stress compared with employees who reported no recent, current or anticipated change (55 percent vs. 22 percent), and more than four times as likely to report experiencing physical health symptoms at work (34 percent vs. 8 percent)."[36]

What makes it stressful to cope with change in a work environment is the feeling that you suddenly have *increased* responsibilities (learning the new technology or adapting to the new market conditions), while at the same time you also have *decreased* power and authority (we often don't get to choose the changes that come to us).

A great leader works at creating a positive atmosphere that allows everyone to do their best and contribute to a successful response to the change.

A few pointers for successful leadership in changing times, and for effective crisis response

As a longtime leader in my own career, and as a student of leadership who has observed dozens of leaders up close and personal, and interviewed hundreds more, I can tell you there's no secret in practicing successful leadership skills in changing times, or in a crisis.

---

36   American Psychological Association, "Change at Work Linked to Employee Stress, Distrust and Intent to Quit, New Survey Finds." May 24, 2017. *www.apa.org/news/press/releases/2017/05/ employee-stress*

In leadership, as in many other areas of life, the hard part isn't knowing what to do -- the hard part is actually doing it.

But there's good news. If you can step back and see the big picture, and understand how all the pieces of this puzzle fit together, and if you realize how and why practicing these skills can result in success on many levels – personal, professional, organizational, even societal -- then it definitely becomes easier cope with changing times. It can even make it a little easier to rise to a crisis. Here, then, are some of the tried and true strategies of successful leaders in tough times.

Communicate more often, and share more information

When your organization is facing a challenge and people are concerned about their own futures and the company's future, a good leader reaches out much more frequently to his or her team. The best leaders connect two or three times as often during challenging times, as compared to "normal" times.

Also, when successful leaders reach out, it's not just to mouth platitudes like "Don't worry, everything will be fine." A good leader shares information about the change and gives people a sense of what's happening with the organization, where things are heading, and what's likely to happen next.

If there is bad news, or potentially bad news, don't hide it. Remember, your credibility is your single greatest asset as a leader. Be as candid as possible, yet also reassuring as possible.

Tell your team, "Here are some of the things I'm concerned about. Here's what I think might happen and how we can respond if they do happen. And here's why I think if we do A, B, and C, we can reasonably hope for a positive outcome."

By the way, increased communication becomes even more important when your team members find themselves in enforced isolation, such as the pandemic lockdown of 2020. When people work 100% in a virtual or remote environment, there is no hall chatter. There are no friendly, spontaneous chats over the water cooler.

A good leader tries to compensate for the lack of these in-person informal channels, by ramping up the staff meetings, and perhaps also by creating new institutions.

Examples in the age of Zoom include the online coffee break, the afterwork online happy hour, the "Meet Your Team" sessions, the "Lunch and Learn" opportunities – all shared on Zoom, Skype, BlueJean or your organization's communication platform of choice.

Be more visible

In a stressful time or in a crisis, let your followers see you. That means face to face communication – in person if possible, but over a video conferencing service if necessary.

When people in an organization are under stress, it's not good enough to get email memos from the boss, or even to hear a disembodied voice. People crave human connection at all times, but they need it even more in difficult times. So walk the halls, pat people on the back, or at least turn on your video camera. It makes a difference.

By the way, it can also be a valuable mood-brightener for the leader to make eye to eye contact with followers. When people like and respect each other, their confidence and energy level goes up, just from being in the same room or the same virtual space together. Human beings are social animals, never more so than in difficult situations. We band together for comfort, not just functional efficiency.

When you do share facetime with team members, smile. Be positive. The leader's mood instantly spreads to the entire organization. If the leader is upbeat, the team is upbeat. If the leader is worried or depressed, so is the team.

When Indra Nooyi took over as CEO at PepsiCo, her predecessor said, "I have one word of advice. Every morning when you arrive here at company headquarters, your limo is going to pull up and let you out in front of the main entrance. When you get out of the car, hundreds of PepsiCo employees will be watching you from the windows of our building. They will be waiting to see your body language and the expression on your face. If you look and act confident, they will be reassured and encouraged. If you don't, they'll start worrying and asking what's wrong."

Indra said she took this advice to heart. She made a point of putting on a big show of upbeat optimism every morning when she climbed out of that limo!

Keep a positive attitude. Look for the silver lining

When you hit a brick wall, or it falls on you, this experience doesn't have to be a dead end or a failure. It can be a learning opportunity.

Specifically, a crisis is an opportunity for you as the leader – and for all of your team members -- to come up with new ways of doing business, to be creative, to think outside the box, to think about changing circumstances and how they affect old, established business models. Many good new ideas and practices come out of this.

Be a "change agent" and stay in "perpetual learning mode"

The single best recipe I ever heard for coping with change, originated from Nobel Prize-winning physicist Dennis Gabor. His writing provided the original basis for an idea that is now cited constantly:

$$\textit{"The best way to predict the future is to help create it."}[37]$$

What does that mean, exactly?

It means <u>make change your friend</u>. All successful leaders cope well with change, but great leaders don't just passively sit back,

---

[37]   In his 1962 book "Inventing the Futures," Gabor actually said, "The future cannot be predicted, but futures can be invented." Over the years this line has been quoted and requoted, and in the process has been modified several times until it reached the form we know today. See https://quoteinvestigator.com/2012/09/27/invent-the-future/

waiting for change to happen, and then react to it. They take a pro-active approach.

The best leaders are "change agents." They make it an ongoing, regular habit to plan change -- initiate change – take charge of change – execute change -- and even, to the extent possible, control change.

This proactive approach is not a panacea for every challenge, of course. It won't end a global recession, or make a pandemic go away. Launching a new product or a new policy usually can't repair a damaged market or replace a lost asset overnight.

But if you can adopt this proactive attitude that "change is your friend" and make it a fundamental part of your leadership culture, then you and your followers will enjoy a huge advantage over everyone else – even when changes arrive that you did not want or expect.

When those changes come, you'll already be experienced with adapting to change. You'll be in a perpetual learning mode, which is one of the key strategies for successfully coping with change. And emotionally, you'll be in your comfort zone, facing "just one more change" in a long series of changes that were often embraced voluntarily. You and your organization will not be totally thrown for a loop.

Keep your perspective, and remember that humor is a powerful tool

Wise leaders know there is a difference between being serious (which is good) and being grim (which is bad). Successful leaders understand the incredible value of humor in getting people relaxed, breaking the tension, breaking the ice, lowering blood pressure, and giving everyone a chance to "show up" as their best selves.

Humor is also a subversive, clever mind trick because it's about seeing things from a fresh, surprising new perspective. That is exactly what leaders and organizations need to do, whenever they're undergoing a challenge or facing a crisis.

"Just make sure [your humor is] inclusive and respectful," says organizational psychologist Nick Tasler. "A good rule of thumb is that other people's strife is no laughing matter, but your own struggles can be a source of comedic gold."[38]

What about claims that humor is "inappropriate" in a crisis, or that jokes are "not fitting" for certain environments?

There is a simple answer to that. Two answers, in fact.

Answer number one: The most moving funerals I've ever attended included both laughter and tears (sometimes both at once). The people giving the eulogies told wonderful stories about the departed, stories that revealed their personalities in an endearing – and often humorous – way.

If we can laugh at funerals, we can certainly laugh in any leadership situation, no matter how tough.

Answer number two: Three of America's greatest Presidents -- Abraham Lincoln, Franklin Delano Roosevelt, and Ronald Reagan -- were all famous for their wit and humor, even in the darkest times. If these three leaders could keep joking in the middle of the Civil War, World War II and the Cold War, then all of us can definitely take a moment to find a bit of levity now and then – even in a business crisis or a family crisis.

We can especially find a role for humor if it's in good taste and it helps us and our teams get through a tough period – and I assure you, it will!

Tomorrow's Leader in the home stretch: you're ready to lead

We have come a long way together on this journey to leadership. We started with the idea that *all leadership begins with self-leadership*, and that leadership is a skill to be learned – not a magical gift from the gods.

---

38   Nick Tasler, "How to Get Better at Dealing with Change," *Harvard Business Review,* September 21, 2016. *https://hbr.org/2016/09/how-to-get-better-at-dealing-with-change*

We saw why successful leadership relies on making one small step at a time, not trying to rush from here to Mars in a hurry-up expedition.

We revealed the 10 most common roadblocks to success, and we discussed the tremendous value of mentors in helping us see (and overcome) our own blind spots.

We explored the amazing power of having an inspiring vision, because "every great path leads to a great destination." We talked about the keys to successful decision-making, and how to balance gut instinct with rational analysis for the best chance at a successful outcome.

We talked about how leaders will meet many different people on their journey, requiring a versatile approach – including the ability to employ more than just one or two styles of leadership.

We established the indispensable nature of *trust* as the corner-stone of successful leadership, and a vital part of a healthy culture of leadership.

We embraced "the beauty of simplicity" and examined how even the most complex goal or concept can be broken down into a series of simple, achievable, easily-understood steps or ideas.

Finally, in this chapter, we have tackled the greatest leadership test of all: coping with the pressures of constant, unpredictable change and the challenge of meeting a crisis.

Now it's time for you to start applying these principles. You may have already begun doing so.

If so, I know that you will continue to make progress – because, *if you're reading these words now, you have already demonstrated a level of passion and commitment that are the ultimate fuel for leadership success.*

THIS IS YOUR TIME TO STEP UP AND BECOME TOMORROW'S LEADER! Congratulations, and best of luck on this ever-exciting journey. I have every confidence that you will make both of us proud!

The journey of leadership never ends - and I'm here for you every step of the way

Together, we can make it our lifelong mission to keep growing and keep learning the art of leadership. I urge you to join me!

Maybe you can tell I'm passionate about leadership. So passionate that I have devoted decades to studying it and practicing it.

What's more, I fully expect to continue expanding my "leadership education" and working at improving my own leadership skills for the rest of my life. I hope you will adopt this goal, too.

One thing I've learned is that *we never learn it all*. When it comes to leadership, there is always a new mountain to climb -- a new skill to master -- a new destination to advance toward. That never-ending challenge is what makes the quest of leadership exciting.

As the poet said, "A man's reach should exceed his grasp, or what's a heaven for?"

I'm here to support your personal journey of leadership

Together, we've covered 12 of the most important skills on the journey of leadership in this book. Now it's time for your personal exploration to begin. But take heart -- you don't have to make this journey alone!

I've made it an important part of my mission to continually share with you the ongoing lessons that I'm learning about leadership – through podcasts, YouTube videos, public talks, blog posts, and consulting.

Please think of these as "resources for the road ahead." Here's where you can find me:

- Follow me on Twitter: (*Give twitter handle*)
- Follow me on Linked In: *www.linkedin.com/in/johnlaurito/*
- Sign up for my Apple podcast address: https://podcasts.apple.com/us/podcast/tomorrows-leader/id1498446688
- Check out my YouTube channel:https://www.youtube.com/channel/UCGJXdFTRgrIIW3WcXm2v83g/featured

These resources are absolutely free, and they're growing week by week!

Of course, if you or your organization would like to engage me to speak to your group, or to provide consulting (either one-on-one or to a leadership team), I'm available for that too.

Feel free to message me on Linked In, or email me at:

john@lauritogroup.com

Final thought: the heart of leadership

Allow me to share one final insight about the ultimate importance of leadership. Have you ever wondered what makes this field so exciting and deeply rewarding for so many people?

Yes, for some people, leadership is about the age-old search for power and money. But while these self-seeking egotists receive much of the attention, in my opinion they are not the truest examples of what genuine leadership is all about.

The truth is, there are tens of millions of "servant leaders" all over the world who get a far bigger kick out of helping others reach their potential, than from enhancing the leader's personal prestige or polishing their self-image.

The greatest leaders aren't looking in the mirror. They're looking ahead to the horizon.

For the best leaders, the rewards of leadership have more in common with being a great parent or a great teacher, than with being a "star" or a kingpin.

True leadership is not about hogging the spotlight or grabbing the brass ring. It's about what you can give, not what you can get.

I believe this is why the relationship between leaders and communities is one of the most powerful and important human dynamics of all. Leadership can be as passionate as romantic love -- as altruistic as the parent-child bond -- and as exciting as being reunited with a long-lost family member.

This deep human connection makes leadership a privilege and a necessity for all of us. I am totally confident that you have a leader inside of you – and now it's time to unleash your leadership upon the world.

The next stage in your lifelong journey of leadership lies before you. Once again, the road is open. The flag is up...

Ladies and gentlemen, start your engines!

Your 30-day Game Plan for a strong start

Each day for the next 30 days, take just 1 simple action step... or focus on 1 inspirational idea to become Tomorrow's Leader

Inspiration is more precious than gold. Inspiration can change the world and transform your life. Gold just changes your balance sheet.

If you're revved up by the idea of becoming Tomorrow's Leader, then you possess that precious treasure known as inspiration. Use it or lose it! NOW is the time to take advantage of this powerful emotional energy and drive. Don't wait until the excitement dies down, and don't allow distractions to drain away your resolve. Leverage your inspiration right away!

Here are 30 quick, simple things you can do each day in your first month on the road to great leadership. Most of these suggestions take just 5 or 10 minutes at most.

Some are concrete, physical actions. Many are "framing" exercises, points to ponder, and decisions that will help you define your ultimate destination, get you moving in the right direction, and keep the momentum going.

The first step is the most crucial, so I urge you to get started as soon as possible. Tomorrow is better than next week; today is better than tomorrow; and now, this minute, is the best of all.

Make a commitment to follow this 30-day Game Plan and take your first step immediately!

Day 1
Create Your Vision

Take 5 or 10 minutes to ask yourself, "Where do I want to be in 3 years? What does it look like?" Be as specific as possible. Jot it down in just 25 or 50 words maximum.

Don't worry if it isn't perfect; you will probably evolve this vision many times as you progress down the road to becoming Tomorrow's Leader.

But by putting your vision into actual words, on a page or a screen, you make that vision real. It gives you something concrete that you're committing to work toward. Assuming that you purchased a physical copy of this book, you can write notes about your vision here on this page, so you'll always have it in this copy of *Tomorrow's Leader*:

_____

_____

_____

_____

_____

_____

_____

_____

_____

_____

Day 2
Make Your Vision Compelling

Take 5 or 10 minutes to jot down something about the impact of reaching your vision. How does it feel when you get there? You can answer in just 2 or 3 words.

How will others around you benefit when you reach your goal? How will you benefit?

Feel free to make this part of your vision as extensive as you like, but don't get hung up on elaborate narratives. This isn't a writing exercise; it's a feeling exercise.

_____

_____

_____

_____

_____

_____

_____

_____

_____

_____

_____

_____

_____

Day 3
Share Your Vision with Someone

Now take that compelling vision and describe it to someone. A friend, a colleague, or best of all, a mentor. Ask for their feedback. Make sure it's someone you respect, and who can respect a confidence from you.

Who will you share your vision with?

What was their reaction?

_____

_____

_____

_____

_____

_____

_____

_____

_____

_____

_____

_____

_____

Day 4
Solicit Feedback from a Trusted Source

Ask someone you trust to give you the straight scoop, "What can I do to become a better leader? What should I start doing? Keep doing? Stop doing?"

Who did you ask?

What did they say?

_____

_____

_____

_____

_____

_____

_____

_____

_____

_____

_____

_____

_____

_____

_____

Day 5
Give Feedback to Another Person

Give someone in your circle a bit of feedback on something that involves a shared goal or a common responsibility. Remember to be specific and constructive.

If there is any critical feedback, "sandwich" the negatives between two positives.

Who did you give feedback to? What was the essence of your message?

How did it go?

_____

_____

_____

_____

_____

_____

_____

_____

_____

_____

_____

_____

Day 6
Have a "Difficult" Conversation

What is a "difficult" conversation? It's the one you have been putting off.

Remember to use the Whole Message Model: Observations, Thoughts, Feelings, Actions.

Who did you speak to? How did it go?

In just 2-10 words, what were the Observations, Thoughts, Feelings and Actions prompted by this conversation?

_____

_____

_____

_____

_____

_____

_____

_____

_____

_____

_____

_____

Day 7
Manage Your Clock
(time management step 1)

Today, be deliberate about controlling your schedule or your priorities and be aware of how you allocate time to them, according to their importance.

What are your 3 most important "big rocks" – the 3 biggest obstacles in the road that you need to remove or go around, in order to reach an immediate goal?

Jot them down before starting your day, and schedule when you will tackle them.

My 3 "Big Rocks" for Today:

Accomplished? _____

Accomplished? _____

Accomplished? _____

Day 8
Manage Your Calendar
(time management step 2)

How do you define a successful day? Or, how will you define today in terms of success requirements?

How do you define a successful week?

Take 5 minutes to jot down a brief "yardstick" that you'll use to define a successful day and week.

For me a successful day will be:

_____

_____

_____

_____

A successful week will be:

_____

_____

_____

_____

Day 9
Identify Your Biggest Time Drains & Time Enablers
(time management step 3)

Who or what are your biggest distractions or time-intensive detours that take your focus away from your daily or weekly goals, or on dealing with the Big Rocks in your road?

_____

_____

_____

Who or what are your 2 or 3 biggest time-savers – the people or factors that help you be most productive and focused?

It might be something as simple as creating a daily "To Do" list. Or it could be a great team member who helps keep you on track.

My biggest "Time Savers" are:

_____

_____

_____

Also, quickly ask yourself: What time of day am I most productive and focused, and why? Write it down. Least productive? Write it down!

Most: _____

Least: _____

Day 10
Build a "Model Week"
(time management step 4)

Now bring all your previous Time Management steps together

Create a "Model Week" incorporating what you learned from the last 3 days of action steps and focus points.

	Mon	Tues	Wed	Thurs	Fri	Sat/Sun
6am						
7am						
8am						
9am						
10am						
11am						
noon						
1pm						
2pm						
3pm						
4pm						
5pm						
6pm						
7pm						
8pm						

Day 11
Zero in on Your Core Values

Complete the values exercise in the Appendix and identify your top 3-5 Core Values. Write them here:

_____

_____

_____

_____

_____

_____

_____

_____

_____

_____

_____

_____

_____

Day 12
Matching Values and Actions

Take 5 minutes to ask yourself a crucial question: "Are my Core Values reflected in my Model Week?"

For example, if health is a Core Value, have you set aside time for healthy activities? If family is a Core Value, have you marked off an appropriate amount of time that you will not compromise?

If excellence is a Core Value, does your Model Week build in any time to develop your skills and expertise? Jot down your assessment here:

_____

_____

_____

_____

_____

Now take 5 minutes and go back to your Model Week, making any needed changes to ensure that it faithfully reflects your Core Values.

_____

_____

_____

_____

_____

Day 13
Look in the Mirror

This is a challenging exercise, but it can also be an invaluable source of insight and yes, even inspiration. Ask yourself... What was the _worst_ decision you have made in the last 3 years? Briefly jot it down (preferably in 1 sentence).

_____

_____

What caused you to make this decision? (Again, try to answer in 1 sentence).

_____

_____

What emotions were present when you made this decision? (Just a few words will do – hope, fear, pride, confidence, panic?)

_____

_____

Was the decision in alignment with your Core Values? Why or why not?

_____

_____

Day 14
Learn from Your Own Success

Now let's flip the script on yesterday's focus point. What was the _best_ decision you've made over the past 3 years? Why was it the best?

_____

_____

What caused you to make this decision? (Again, try to answer in 1 sentence).

_____

_____

What emotions were present when you made this decision? (Just a few words will do).

_____

_____

Was the decision in alignment with your Core Values? Why or why not?

_____

_____

Day 15
Evaluate an Upcoming Major Decision

Think about a big decision that you will have to make in the near future. Briefly job down what the decision is, and why is it a major decision? What impact will it have?

_____

_____

Now use the "10-10-10 Rule" to evaluate one possible way to go with your upcoming decision. If you choose that option, how will you feel in 10 minutes?

_____

_____

How will you feel in 10 months?

_____

_____

How will you feel 10 years after making that decision?

_____

_____

How does each option for this decision align with your Core Values, and with your organization's Core Values?

_____

_____

Day 16
Take an "Instant Personal Inventory"
(self-awareness step 1)

Self-awareness is a critical ingredient of excellent leadership. Here's a useful tool that can help you gain some valuable self-awareness insights in just 1 minute.

To start with, "freeze" yourself physically and mentally, right this instant. Now take a moment to examine what's going on with you, as if you were an objective third party looking at yourself. Answer 3 questions:

What am I thinking? What am I saying to myself?

_____

_____

How am I feeling? What emotions are present with me?

_____

_____

What am I doing with my body, and how am I feeling physically?

_____

_____

Once you become aware of yourself on these 3 levels, does it change how you view your surroundings? Your immediate focus or goals? Your strategy for dealing with your environment?

_____

_____

Day 17
Facing Your Discomfort Zones
(self-awareness step 2)

Take just 30 seconds to think about 1 thing that you've been afraid to do, or reluctant to handle, because it makes you uncomfortable.

What is this situation or issue?

_____

_____

_____

How long have you been delaying dealing with this issue?

_____

_____

_____

Now here's the tough part. What has been your "self-talk" regarding this issue? What have you been telling yourself? (Be specific).

_____

_____

_____

Congratulations! Just by answering these questions, you have done 75% of the work required to tackle this issue successfully and deal with it in an effective way that you can be proud of. (As you'll see with tomorrow's focus point).

Day 18
Reframe Your Thinking
(self-awareness step 3)

Yesterday you identified an issue that you felt uncomfortable about dealing with. Now use one of the two techniques to reframe your thinking and change your self-talk on this issue.

The Turnaround Technique: Look at the situation from another person's perspective. If one of your mentors or admired colleagues were facing this issue, how would they handle it? Or, what might they say about how you're thinking of handling it?

_____

_____

_____

_____

_____

The Dispute Technique: Take 1 minute to jot down 2 or 3 facts that contradict your negative self-talk. They can be facts about you or about the situation.

_____

_____

_____

_____

_____

Day 19
Expand Your Comfort Zone
(self-awareness step 4)

Now that you have reframed your self-talk in a more constructive, and hopefully a more objective, light – it's time to take action!

Whatever it is that you've been putting off, take the first major step to start dealing with it. Make that call, set the appointment, start putting together the information required to make that big decision … or, if you already have the information, then make the decision.

You will feel much better afterward…if you keep in mind yesterday's action steps to Reframe the Problem and Dispute the Negative Interpretation.

If you don't feel great, go back and do yesterday's exercise again!

How did it go, taking the step that was uncomfortable?

_____

_____

_____

_____

How do you feel now?

_____

_____

_____

_____

Day 20
Add Tools to Your "Leadership Toolbox"
(step 1)

Go back and review the diagram on the 6 basic Leadership Styles earlier in this book.

Identify the leadership style that you believe is your dominant, go-to mode or technique.

What kind of leader do you naturally gravitate toward being?

_____

_____

_____

Now identify two other leadership styles that you feel would make you a more effective leader if used on occasion. What are they, and in what situations would you employ them?

1st leadership style and application:

_____

_____

_____

2nd leadership style and application:

_____

_____

_____

Day 21
Add Tools to Your "Leadership Toolbox"
(step 2)

Take 5 minutes to think back over your past month. Can you identify 1 or 2 opportunities where it would have been effective to use one of the leadership styles that you want to master?

_____

_____

_____

_____

_____

_____

Let's do a "thought experiment." If you had deployed one of those new leadership styles, how might the outcome have been different?

_____

_____

_____

_____

_____

_____

_____

Day 22
Add Tools to Your "Leadership Toolbox"
(step 3)

Take 5 minutes to think ahead to your next week or two. Can you point to some specific events or occasions when, where and how you can try out these leadership styles in the upcoming period?

_____

_____

_____

_____

_____

What will it look like and sound like, when you put one of these leadership styles into action?

_____

_____

_____

_____

_____

Try to use one of these styles over the next week if you can. I'll ask you about them on Day 29!

Day 23
Becoming More Aware of How You're Influenced by Others

Just off the top of your head, identify the person or persons who have the most influence on your own leadership. How do they influence you?

_____

_____

Who are the 5 people you spend the most time with, and how do those 5 people impact you?

_____

_____

Are these 5 people helping you grow? In what ways? Or, if there is something missing, what are these 5 not giving you that you need or want?

_____

_____

Are these 5 people the right ones to have in your "inner circle"? If yes, how can you maximize their influence? In no, then what changes, if any, do you need to make?

_____

_____

Day 24
Becoming More Aware of Your Own Influence on Others

One of the most important roles of a great leader is to help develop and nurture leadership in others.

Are you developing leaders among the people around you? What leaders are you developing, and in what ways and areas you developing them?

_____

_____

_____

_____

_____

_____

_____

How can you be more effective in helping to develop Tomorrow's Leaders around you?

Take 3 minutes and jot down just ONE THING that would help them develop their own leadership faster, over the next 6 months.

_____

Day 25
Strengthen Your Self-Development
(step 1)

What steps are you taking to develop your own leadership? (Aside from reading this book.)

_____

_____

_____

_____

_____

Are you currently working with a trusted advisor or Executive Coach?

What 1 or 2 areas are you most interested in developing, where a coach may be able to help you work on those skills?

_____

_____

_____

_____

_____

Day 26
Strengthen Your Self-Development
(step 2)

How do you want people to describe you as a leader? What would you want them to say?

_____

_____

_____

_____

_____

_____

If someone asked the people around you to describe you as a leader, what might they say? Be honest!

_____

_____

_____

_____

_____

_____

_____

Day 27
Strengthen Your Self-Development
(step 3)

Take 1 step today to accelerate your development or a leader.

Interview / hire a coach

_____

_____

_____

_____

Enroll in a leadership development program

Join a leadership "leadership mastermind" group

_____

_____

_____

_____

Other

_____

_____

_____

_____

Day 28
Work on Delegating Tasks

Identify one thing you are currently doing that someone else can do at least 80% as well as you can.

_____

_____

_____

_____

_____

_____

_____

Who can you delegate that task to?

_____

Go ahead – let the other person try handling that task. How did it go?

_____

_____

_____

_____

Day 29
Add Tools to Your "Leadership Toolbox"
(step 4)

On Day 22, you decided to test out 1 or 2 other leadership styles.

What happened?

_____

_____

_____

_____

What would you do differently next time?

_____

_____

_____

_____

Great job! Keep stretching yourself to achieve more leadership versatility and flexibility, because there are few ways to grow faster as a leader.

Remember, only 1% of leaders routinely use 4 or more styles of leadership. Every time you become even a little bit conversant with using a new leadership style, you are on your way to joining the upper tier of leadership.

Day 30
Make a Promise to Yourself

Congratulations. If you faithfully completed the previous 29 days of action steps and focus points, then you have made a tremendously strong start in your journey to becoming *Tomorrow's Leader.*

From this point forward, it's critical that you take ongoing, specific steps to <u>continue developing your leadership skills</u>. I urge you to spend some time now – today -- to think about which principles and lessons from this book you can apply to the next phase of your journey. Then, distill them into 3-5 "action steps" that will put those principles into practice.

Finally, and most importantly, <u>make a commitment to yourself</u> that you will take those actions over the next 30 days. There is a great power in making a formal promise to yourself, and now is an excellent time to start learning how to use that power! So complete this thought: *"I am committing to take the following steps in the next 30 days..."*

Action Step 1: _____

Action Step 2: _____

Action Step 3: _____

Action Step 4: _____

Action Step 5: _____

I have written this book because I care about you, about your success at becoming one of *Tomorrow's Leaders,* and about your happiness. I am here to help. If you would like more information on any aspect of the *Tomorrow's Leader* philosophy, or where you can find my podcast, speaking schedule or coaching availabilities, feel free to contact me at:

John@lauritogroup.com

www.johnlaurito.com

Appendix

Values Exercise

Take a few minutes now to identify your values. Use the following list to think about what you value most in life. Place checkmarks next to all of the words below that are important to you. Then circle the 15 that are most important and meaningful to you.

CORE VALUES IDENTIFICATION LIST

❑ Achievement	❑ Fairness	❑ Order
❑ Advancement & Promotion	❑ Fame	❑ Personal Development
❑ Adventure	❑ Family Happiness	❑ Personal Expression
❑ Affection	❑ Fast Living	❑ Playfulness
❑ Arts	❑ Fast-paced Work	❑ Pleasure
❑ Autonomy	❑ Financial Gain	❑ Power
❑ Challenging Problems	❑ Freedom	❑ Privacy
❑ Change & Variety	❑ Friendship	❑ Purity
❑ Close Relationships	❑ Growth	❑ Quality
❑ Community	❑ Health	❑ Recognition
❑ Competence	❑ Helping Others	❑ Relationships
❑ Competition	❑ Helping Society	❑ Religion
❑ Completion	❑ Honesty	❑ Reputation
❑ Cooperation	❑ Independence	❑ Responsibility & Accountability
❑ Collaboration	❑ Influencing Others	❑ Safety & Security
❑ Country	❑ Inner Harmony	❑ Self Respect
❑ Creative Expression	❑ Integrity	❑ Serenity
❑ Decisiveness	❑ Intellectual Status	❑ Service
❑ Democracy	❑ Involvement	❑ Sophistication
❑ Diversity	❑ Job Tranquillity	❑ Spirituality
❑ Ecological Awareness	❑ Knowledge	❑ Stability
❑ Economic Security	❑ Leadership	❑ Status
❑ Effectiveness	❑ Location	❑ Time Freedom
❑ Efficiency	❑ Loyalty	❑ Truth
❑ Equality	❑ Meaningful Work	❑ Wealth
❑ Ethical Practice	❑ Merit	❑ Wisdom
❑ Excellence	❑ Money	❑ Work Alone
❑ Excitement	❑ Nature	❑ Work on Frontiers
❑ Expertise	❑ Openness	❑ Work with Others
❑ _____	❑ _____	❑ _____

CORE VALUES IDENTIFICATION WORKSHEET

Write those 15 values from the Core Values Identification List in the left-hand column below. After you have written your 15 values in the left-hand hand column, select from that list the 10 values that are the most important to you. Finally, narrow it down to your 5 core values.

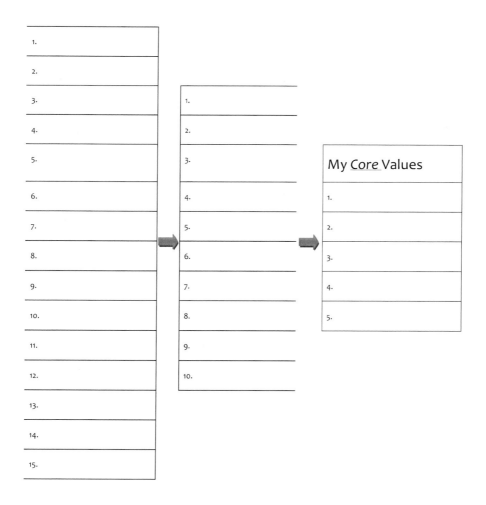